PRAISE FOR *UNEXPLAINA...*

...rica Wiggenhorn. The girl unpacks a spiritual truth like nobody's business. But this ...ime? It's personal. Like "practically feel the dust-grit from Jesus' sandals" personal. It does get heart-personal when we look so closely at the cultural, historical, and religious background of our Jewish-Rabbi-Savior. Can't NOT be changed by this fabulous study of Luke's gospel.

RHONDA RHEA, TV personality, author of 15 books, including *Fix Her Upper, Messy to Meaningful,* and the award-winning *Turtles in the Road*

If you long to get to know Jesus more intimately than you've ever experienced Him before, I implore you to call some friends and do this study as a group. Bible teacher Erica Wiggenhorn skillfully guides her readers to an understanding of the mystery and wonder of the most fascinating man you'll ever know—Jesus. You'll laugh. You'll cry. You'll be amazed as you encounter Him in an up close and personal way. This is a Bible study that will transform your life.

CAROL KENT, speaker and author *He Holds My Hand: Experiencing God's Presence and Protection*

Unexplainable Jesus: Rediscovering the God You Thought You Knew is biblically robust, but Erica also writes in a winsome and transparent style that makes you feel like she's just talking to you over a cup of coffee! It is so refreshing to read her insights and join in the "Aha!" moments when Scripture comes alive.

MATT VALENCIA, Lead Pastor of ReGeneration Church

The best teaching comes from experience. Going through this study, it is obvious that Erica has had an experience with Jesus. She didn't just create a Bible study; she mapped out a journey through the life of Christ. At the end of the forty days, not only will you have a very well-informed picture of the life of Christ, you will have had your faith stretched, your heart encouraged, and your own experience with Jesus.

RYAN NUNEZ, Lead Pastor of Palm Valley Church, Arizona

Wonderful word pictures along with accurate historical research, coupled with Erica's easy-to-read and comprehensive writing style, makes *Unexplainable Jesus* understandable! I didn't want to put this study down!

MARK W. RICE, Senior Pastor of Mesa Baptist Church; President of Southwest Church Connection

Jesus asked, "Who do you say that I am?" Each of us needs a time to pause, ponder and walk with Jesus in a way that helps us get to know Him better. Erica has provided a wonderful opportunity in this beautiful book, *Unexplainable Jesus*.

PAM FARREL, author of 47 books, including *Discovering Hope in the Psalms*, *Discovering Joy in Philippians*, and *A Couple's Journey with God*

Erica Wiggenhorn brilliantly brought me through a clear yet multidimensional understanding of God's love and redemption story through the gospel of Luke. *Unexplainable Jesus* radically transformed my personal walk with Jesus by revealing exciting, transformative insights of how God used—*and uses*—people for His glory through our individual stories. Whether you have known Jesus for most of your life or you are still finding out who He is, you will encounter a new personal, praiseworthy, and compassionate understanding of our beautiful Savior—Jesus!

MELINDA WOCHNER, Women's Director, Grace Community Church

You are going to be blessed processing this new study of Luke by Erica Wiggenhorn— *Unexplainable Jesus*! Drawing from the pages of Luke, the early church historian, Erica helps draw out the real Jesus who changed the world through His life and changed the course of human history by His death and resurrection. But the blessing will come not merely from the information that Erica shares, but by the transformation that the Holy Spirit will do in your life as you engage the life of the Son of God. Erica's writing style and insights will serve as launching points for the Holy Spirit in your heart to continue the process of changing you to be more like Jesus (2 Cor. 3:18).

STEVE ENGRAM, pastor at Desert Springs Community Church; Executive Director, Southwest Church Connection

Unexplainable Jesus takes the gospel of Luke and presents it in language that is compelling and easily understood. Erica's personal and practical style invite you into an exciting relationship with Jesus, to grasp His deep, abiding, and relentless love for you, not just a bunch of head knowledge. If you are ready to sit at the feet of Jesus and fall more in love with Him than ever, this study is for you!

DEBBIE GRIBAUSKAS, founder, Beyond Fear to Freedom, Phoenix, AZ

unexplainable
JESUS

REDISCOVERING THE GOD YOU THOUGHT YOU KNEW

AN 8-WEEK BIBLE STUDY OF *LUKE*

ERICA WIGGENHORN

MOODY PUBLISHERS

CHICAGO

Published in association with the literary agency of The Steve Laube Agency, 24 W. Camelback Rd, A-635, Phoenix, AZ 85013.

Edited by Pamela J. Pugh
Cover and interior design: Erik M. Peterson
Cover illustration of Jesus and cross copyright © 2018 by Prixel Creative / Lightstock (211095). All rights reserved.
Author photo: Suzanne Busta

Library of Congress Cataloging-in-Publication Data

Names: Wiggenhorn, Erica, author.
Title: Unexplainable Jesus : rediscovering the God you thought you knew : an
   8-week Bible study of the Gospel of Luke / Erica Wiggenhorn.
Description: Chicago : Moody Publishers, 2019. | Includes bibliographical
   references and index.
Identifiers: LCCN 2019000178 (print) | LCCN 2019016638 (ebook) | ISBN
   9780802497765 (ebook) | ISBN 9780802419095 (alk. paper)
Subjects: LCSH: Bible. Luke--Textbooks.
Classification: LCC BS2596 (ebook) | LCC BS2596 .W543 2019 (print) | DDC
   226.4/0071--dc23
LC record available at https://lccn.loc.gov/2019000178

ISBN: 978-0-8024-1909-5

We hope you enjoy this book from Moody Publishers. Our goal is to provide high-quality, thought-provoking books and products that connect truth to your real needs and challenges. For more information on other books and products written and produced from a biblical perspective, go to www.moodypublishers.com or write to:

Moody Publishers
820 N. LaSalle Boulevard
Chicago, IL 60610

1 3 5 7 9 10 8 6 4 2

Printed in the United States of America

To: Unexplainable Jesus. I pray that You are pleased with this work.

To: All who open these pages. May you fall more in love with Jesus
than you ever thought possible.

CONTENTS

AN UNEXPLAINABLE ENCOUNTER

Peter hoisted the heavy net out onto the water one last time. Wiping the sweat from his brow, he looked back toward the shore and saw his brother Andrew. "Here he comes again with those desert dwellers preaching repentance," Peter muttered. "I understand John the Baptist's message, but if Andrew doesn't get on this boat and help me, he's going to have some real repenting to do!"

The Romans. Some people thought John the Baptist would overthrow the Romans. Maybe he was the Messiah. He had appeared out of the desert, like many said Messiah would. Andrew certainly was caught up in His message. But Peter had fish to catch, a living to earn, taxes to pay. "Andrew! Andrew!" he bellowed. "Get out here and help me!"

Instead, Andrew motioned excitedly for Peter to come to shore. Peter pulled in the net. Still empty. He rolled his eyes and began rowing to shore. Next to Andrew stood a man. An ordinary man, nothing significant about the guy's stature. Rather homely, actually. Simply dressed. But those eyes. Something about that gaze. It locked on Peter, who sensed that this man could see into his very soul. Peter looked at Andrew partially for an explanation and also to divert the man's attention from him, but the man continued to study Peter, and finally spoke. "Come, follow me, and I will make you fishers of men!"

Andrew grinned. Peter instantly knew Andrew's thoughts by merely glancing at his face. Andrew was all in, certain he had found the Messiah. Peter also felt an urge to follow this man. Something in his heart stirred, and he knew he should go. Then doubt. Fear. Who was this man Jesus? Was his brother right about Him? What exactly would it mean to follow Him? Peter met that gaze again, and he could not look away. Somehow in the depth of his soul he knew he had to go with this man. What lay ahead? He had not a clue, but he dropped his heavy net and embraced a new adventure.

Peter's actions seem impulsive, irresponsible even. His whole life he had worked hard, gotten married, done the right thing. What was so unexplainable about Jesus that Peter instinctively knew he should follow? That is the purpose of this study. To encounter Jesus. Or rediscover Him. To gaze in awe at the wonder of His person. To stand bare before Him and be unable to turn away.

Does that excite you? Frighten you? Feel impossible? Peter, a devout Jew, knew the prophecies regarding Messiah. He knew the Scriptures: the psalms, the proverbs, and the prophets. He knew the law of Moses and the history of the kings. But he didn't know Jesus. He thought he knew what to expect, but Jesus surprised him. He did unexplainable things, leaving Peter in awe.

Maybe you and I need a fresh encounter with Jesus. Maybe you need to encounter Him for the first time to figure out who He actually is and what He came to do. Whether you have read about Him, heard about Him, studied Him, or followed Him, He is so profound, mysterious, and wonderful, I guarantee you have not discovered all that He is. I can also guarantee He longs for you to discover more. To draw closer, to follow Him to places unexplainable.

"Peter," Andrew insisted, "we have found the Messiah! He is the one!"

Will you leave behind your daily, run-of-the-mill everyday life and hope for something greater? Will you search for the sacred? Will you test the truth of what you believe about Jesus? Oh, how I hope so!

"Come, follow Me!" bids Jesus.

Like Andrew, I'm all in too. Let's go together, shall we?

MAKING THE MOST OF THIS STUDY

"For he grew up before him like a young plant,
    and like a root out of dry ground;
he had no form or majesty that we should look at him,
    and no beauty that we should desire him.
He was despised and rejected by men,
    a man of sorrows and acquainted with grief;
and as one from whom men hide their faces
    he was despised, and we esteemed him not. . . .

But he was pierced for our transgressions;
    he was crushed for our iniquities;
upon him was the chastisement that brought us peace,
    and with his wounds we are healed.

—a prophecy regarding the Christ, Isaiah 53:2–3; 5

God's ways are unexplainable. Coming clothed in human flesh, He took the form of a man. An ordinary man with nothing formidable or beautiful about His appearance. He came not as a wealthy or educated man, but as a carpenter, working in a small village in the region of Galilee. Nothing about His upbringing would cause us to predict great plans of God regarding His future. We esteemed Him not.

This man "attested to you by God with mighty works and wonders and signs that God did through him in your midst, as you yourselves know—this Jesus, delivered up according to the definite plan and foreknowledge of God, you crucified and killed by the hands of lawless men. God raised him up, loosing the pangs of death, because it was not possible for him to be held by it" (Acts 2:22–24).

This is the man we will encounter. We will behold His mighty wonders. We will marvel at His wisdom and teaching. We will witness His death and resurrection.

And we will make a choice. Will we believe He was pierced for our transgressions? Will we believe this Jesus cannot be held by death and that He has conquered sin? Will we put our faith and trust in this unexplainable Jesus who died that we might live?

And if we do, what does faith in an unexplainable Savior look like?

As Jesus approached Jerusalem, resolutely ready to be crucified for our sins, He posed a poignant question regarding His return:

"When the Son of Man comes, will he find faith on earth?" (Luke 18:8).

Forty days is a common time period referenced throughout Scripture. It was often used as a time of purification and preparation. This study is an invitation to spend the next forty days encountering this unexplainable Jesus. To wrestle through His words and figure out what faith in His person and following Him in your circumstances actually look like.

As we follow this unexplainable rabbi through the dusty roads of Palestine, may He purify our thinking and prepare our hearts to receive all He has for us. May we *know* Jesus, and fall in love with this God we thought we knew, but have now met in a new way.

To maximize your study and allow you to listen to God, begin your time with prayer, inviting the Holy Spirit to speak to you. Also, try to study on a daily basis. This allows ample time to contemplate the content and develop a habit of getting alone with God regularly, strengthening your relationship with Him.

At the beginning of each day's lesson you will encounter a Bible passage and a thematic title. Each lesson should take about twenty to thirty minutes to complete. Begin your study time by reading the passage in its entirety. Read the daily passage aloud. I've used the English Standard Version as my main text, but you may of course use any version you're comfortable with. If you find yourself confused by a question's wording, referencing the English Standard Version for greater clarity should prove helpful. Reading the daily verses will offer a basic overview of that day's Scripture and story before we break it down in greater depth. The more you familiarize yourself with the verses, the more likely you will remember them and allow their truths to penetrate your heart.

Making your way through each daily assignment, you will encounter several questions in blue. These questions can help you stop, pray, collect your thoughts, and write out answers. Writing responses prompts you to slow down and grapple with the Scriptures, and apply them to your life. On certain days, you will notice blue picture frames. These are your invitation to press pause and dwell in the truths presented that day. Draw, journal, doodle, or ponder, allowing the Holy Spirit to speak to you in the quietness of your heart. Bible study is not meant to be a task to complete. Instead, it is an avenue for building a relationship with God. Invest time in your relationship with Him.

Some of the blue questions can also be used in small group discussions. The leader's guide for this study indicates which questions work best for groups. You can access this free resource at www.ericawiggenhorn.com.

A bonus for you, *Come to the Table*, has some extra material that corresponds with the study. This is an optional component in which you can dig more deeply into the Scriptures by making cultural connections with life, customs, and celebrations during the time of Jesus. This not only includes additional historical and cultural information, it also has some fun inclusions like recipes, decorating ideas to celebrate Jewish holidays, and other tips to experience some of Jesus' stories from an eyewitness point of view. This is another free resource that is especially helpful for those leading, facilitating, or hosting a small group through this study. It is also available at www.ericawiggenhorn.com.

For those portions of Luke's gospel not addressed in this workbook, an optional resource, the Unexplainable Jesus Video Series, can be purchased (as DVD or digital download) to view me teaching these passages live.

I am praying for you as you walk this journey. I pray that Jesus will speak to you, transform you by grace, and equip you with the truth of His Word. As you stand alongside Him on the temple steps, rest on the shores of the Sea of Galilee, or travel the dusty desert of Judea, may you rediscover the God you thought you knew in ways unexplainable.

We are ready, Jesus! Increase our faith!

Erica

unexplainable
BEGINNINGS

SETTING THE RECORD STRAIGHT

LUKE 1:1–4

Luke is hands down my favorite New Testament author. Paul describes Luke as "the beloved physician" (Col. 4:14). Luke's scientific mind leaves him presenting the facts logically and articulately. His compassion, as one who cares for the sick, bursts through his writing as he paints his characters in living color, full of emotion.

Maybe it's because I feel like I "get him." I live with a "Luke" of my own. I've been married to a physician for over twenty years. Like Luke, my husband, Jonathan, applauds logic and facts, is extremely detail-oriented, and he is compassionate. He has a heart for the suffering and the downcast. His profession of assessing patients and diagnosing them day in and day out causes him to look beyond the surface and, to discover the heart of an individual, the emotional and spiritual covered by the physical. This is Luke's writing style. He invites us to examine Jesus, not just on the surface, but more deeply—to discover how unexplainable He truly is.

In fact, Luke spent years of his life preparing for this work. He traveled the known world interviewing eyewitnesses of Jesus' miracles and teachings. He collected every written work he could find, checking and cross-checking the accounts, comparing them with those he had interviewed. These journeys no doubt came at great personal cost to himself along with tremendous risk. He had been with Paul in Jerusalem during his arrest (Acts 21:17–36). Later he visited Paul during his imprisonment in Caesarea Philippi. He was shipwrecked with Paul on the way to Rome and was one of few companions during his last imprisonment there (Acts 24:23, 27:1–28:1; 2 Tim. 4:11). (Most scholars think Luke was with Paul from Acts 20 to the end of the narrative because of Luke's repeated usage of the pronouns us/we—see Acts 20:5–7, 13; 21:1, 7,15, etc.)

Luke's investigation and presentation of the facts about Jesus were not compiled in the palatial library in Ephesus. They were formed in prison cells, ships tossing on the open sea, and long, dusty roads of travel between Galilee, Jerusalem, and Judea. The development of his books, Luke and Acts, took at least a decade. Some could say they were his legacy. His crowning achievement written for the glory of his Savior: our unexplainable Jesus.

Read aloud Luke 1:1–4.

According to Luke, how prolific were the writings about Jesus at this time?

What word does Luke use to describe his account of Jesus' life and work (see especially v. 3)?

What was his overarching purpose in writing his account?

The other gospel writers, Matthew, Mark, and John, wrote their gospel accounts out of their own personal experiences. They were eyewitnesses of Jesus' life and work. Matthew and John were His disciples. Mark, also known as John Mark, was a young man during Jesus' life and ministry. His mother had been a devout follower of Jesus and often opened her home in Jerusalem for gatherings of the believers. Their accounts are more biographical in nature, emphasizing different aspects of Jesus' life and teachings. Luke's purpose is more apologetic in nature: "I have taken painstaking measures to ensure you that you indeed hold a reasonable faith. Jesus clearly is the Christ, the promised Messiah, God in human flesh, the Savior of the World" (paraphrasing Luke 1:1–4).

The cultural and historical context during the time Luke constructed his Gospel sheds light on the imminent need for an accurate historical document that would outline the life of Jesus. Several events were happening. First, being nearly thirty years after Jesus' death, many of the eyewitnesses were aging and nearing the end of their lives. James, John's brother, had already been beheaded by Herod, and Peter had been forced to flee Jerusalem. The earthly time left for many of these eyewitnesses was short.

Second, anti-Semitism was escalating in the Roman Empire. The Jews had been expelled from Rome under the Emperor Claudius, and their desire to rebel against Rome was rising. With tensions mounting, who knew how much longer it would be until Jesus' prediction regarding the destruction of Jerusalem might take place? Diligent investigative research was predicated on a peaceful climate in which one was free to travel, gathering needed information and interviewing key people. Furthermore, the ancient orators who held these stories and miracles within their hearts and minds predominantly resided in Palestine. What would happen if this city were decimated by the Romans? Who would be left to pass the stories down to the next generation?

How many of these factors resonated in the forefront of Luke's mind we do not know, but the apostolic age was rapidly coming to a close. And unless an accurate, historical, comprehensive account of the life of Jesus was faithfully preserved, the great message of the gospel was in danger of not being spread, as Jesus had commanded.

Let's take that last statement and make it more personal. Fill in your own statement with your action plan.

Unless I _____

_____,

the message of Jesus might not be spread.

Don't generalize. Be specific. Luke expended great effort researching and writing to keep the message of Jesus from dying out. Maybe you're not even sure what the message of Jesus is yet. Maybe that's why you picked up this book—you're still trying to figure Him out. Well, Luke's gospel is a great place to start! Or maybe you've known Him as your Savior for years, but you've become complacent or less than awestruck of all He has done for you.

Let's pause here and set the record straight in our own line of thinking for a moment. How would you describe Jesus using your own modern-day language and logic?

How confident are you that the Christian faith is indeed a reasonable one? Why do you feel as you do?

As you make your way through Luke's gospel, studying the essence, heart, and works of Jesus Christ, what do you hope to gain?

I may not know all the reasons why you have come to this study book, but this much I do know: Jesus' heart is to reveal Himself to you. His desire is that you know Him, believe Him, and experience the love, peace, joy, and purpose that He longs to give you. He is the one and only. He is both human and divine—God among us. He is unexplainable, because there is no one like Him, nor will there ever be another. And as you open up the gospel of Luke, He bids you, "Come, follow Me!"

UNEXPLAINABLE BEGINNINGS
LUKE 1:5–15

Here begins Luke's historical documentary. It is no wonder then that Luke opens the beginning of the story with the mention of Herod, allowing Theophilus, along with every other reader, to know the exact time frame for the opening scene. Herod is not the primary character in this opening scene, however. It is a devout couple going about their everyday lives, doing their everyday duties, when suddenly God sweeps in and does the unexplainable.

Read aloud Luke 1:5–9.

Who are the main characters in this part of the story, and what is their occupation(s)?

How is their character described?

What is their problem?

What special privilege was Zechariah chosen to do at this time?

During the reign of King David there were twenty-four priestly divisions. Abijah was the head of one of them. There were many more priests than were needed for the care and maintenance of the temple, so King David set up a system where the priests from the different divisions would take turns serving at the temple. When it was not their turn, they would return home to their surrounding villages. Only the chief priests permanently resided within Jerusalem.

Zechariah was serving one of his two-week stints in the temple. While he was there he was chosen by lot, as was the custom instituted by King David, to go into the inner court to burn incense. This was a section of the temple, also called the Holy Place, in which only priests were allowed to enter for specified service. With sixteen to twenty thousand priests in Israel, this was a once-in-a-lifetime opportunity. The incense was offered in conjunction with the morning and evening sacrifices and hours of prayer.

At this time in Israel, barrenness was thought to be a punishment from God upon women. Men were allowed to divorce their barren wives in order to preserve their family line. Yet here we have Zechariah faithfully remaining by Elizabeth's side despite their childlessness, both of them steadfastly serving God despite their sorrow. In the midst of their daily routine, God is ready to sweep in and do the dramatic.

Read aloud Luke 1:11–15.
Who appeared to Zechariah, and how did he respond?

What four things did the messenger tell him in v. 13?

How did he describe John, the child who would be born?

I can't help but imagine Zechariah entering the Holy Place with a reverent fear to begin with. This likely could have been his first time inside this hallowed sanctuary.

The awe of the presence of the Almighty just beyond the veil in the Holy of Holies must have gripped him with wonder. The Holy of Holies held the Ark of the Covenant and above this ark, God's glory dwelt. This section of the temple was only entered once a year by the High Priest on the Day of Atonement, after an intense ritual of ceremonial cleansing and appropriate sacrificial offerings. Within a few feet of where Zechariah stood, the glory of the Almighty rested. Usually the priest would place the incense in the bowls and immediately exit. Not Zechariah. He had a message directly from the Almighty: his prayer has been heard.

Don't you wonder what Zechariah's prayer had been? As a representative of the people of Israel and a devout and upright man, surely his prayers went beyond his own selfish interests. Was it the coming of the Messiah? The repentance of his people before a holy God? Comfort for his wife in her grief and shame?

Herein we see the beauty of God. Within the grand story of the great redemption of the earth through the coming Messiah, we also see the tender mercy of God answering a man's innermost prayer. Could it be that Zechariah outwardly prayed for his people and God's promises to be fulfilled and only inwardly yearned for a child? Yet, God heard this unspoken desire of his heart and in His marvelous way, He answered all prayers through the miraculous birth of one life: John.

John, whose name means "the Lord is gracious."

Do you have inner desires within your heart that you have never openly expressed to God?

Or maybe you expressed them to Him long ago, but have since quit asking Him, thinking the time has passed for Him to answer?

What does the story of Zechariah and Elizabeth teach us about God's timing?

What does it mean to you in this moment to be affirmed that God hears your prayer?

Zechariah was faithful, yet he still doubted. But God answered his prayer. In His time. In His way. How often it seems that the story of Zechariah repeats itself throughout the pages of Scripture. People faithfully going about their lives, doing their duty, following God day in and day out and then God suddenly comes in and invites them to do something unexplainable.

Elisha dutifully tending his father's farm and Elijah shows up and throws his prophetic mantle upon him.

Timothy honoring his mother, serving in the local synagogue and Paul comes to town, making him a missionary.

James and John tending nets in their father's fishing boat and Jesus says, "Come! Follow Me!"

Ruth honoring her mother-in-law and becoming the great-grandmother of the great King David of Israel.

Esther, growing and learning under her cousin Mordecai, becomes queen of Persia, saving her people from an evil plot.

Zechariah and Elizabeth devoutly serving God in Judea, visited by an angel, and told they would parent a mighty prophet.

I call these encounters Kingdom Interruptions. God interrupts this everyday life to do something unexplainable.

Now it's your turn:

_____, daily _____
(your name)   (your predominant activities)

_____.

What might your kingdom interruption be?

Could it be a vocation like Elisha and Timothy?

Could it be a volunteer position or a cause like James and John?

Could it be a biological legacy like Ruth and Elizabeth?

Could it be something you would never choose for yourself, but God will call you to as He did Esther?

Could it be that hidden yearning in your heart?

God has heard your prayer, dear one. Do not be afraid. Maybe you'd like to pour out some of your emotions below.

WEEK 1 | DAY 3
THE SPIRT OF ELIJAH AND THE SPIRIT OF GOD
LUKE 1:16–38

I wonder how Zechariah felt regarding the words the angel was speaking. It would be almost too much to take in, wouldn't it? We adopted our son the day he was born, and he was quite ill from the start. He had to stay in the hospital the first week of his life while the doctors ran test after test. The first night after his birth was horrific. He seized and screamed until he fell asleep for two minutes and then it would begin all over again. The nurses told me the only thing I could do was swaddle him as tightly as I could and clutch him securely to my chest. By the morning my arms throbbed and my heart was broken. My saving grace was the presence of my mother-in-law by our side. A nurse for over twenty years, she was the calming presence I needed to not lose it in rage that others' choices would cause him such harm. How long would this last?

The following night I went home to be with our daughter, and my husband stayed with his mom and our son. I feared how the night would unfold. All I could do was pray. The next morning my mother-in-law called and told me how they had the most amazing nurse that night. Her name was Christina. She said she worked with babies like our Nathan all the time and seemed to know exactly what to do. She was able to calm him down and get him to sleep for more than just a couple of minutes at a time. I got in the car and drove to the hospital eager to meet her.

When I laid eyes on Christina, she was not at all what I had expected. She had long gray hair, kind of frizzy, parted in the middle, and wore all-white scrubs, which was a bit odd for a labor and delivery nurse. There was nothing beautiful about her appearance, but her eyes were pools of the purest blue, and I felt as though I could drown in the peace they reflected. She smiled faintly at me and took my hand. She

In my humanness, after waiting so long for a child, I would attempt to protect him from every heartache and difficulty the world would throw at him. Since he was their only son, I imagine Elizabeth and Zechariah were also tempted to try and overprotect him from any danger. But John could not be coddled; he had to be physically strong. He had to be instructed. He had to face difficult things and become courageous, depending on God and not only his parents in order to fulfill the mission God had planned for him.

The truth is that every one of us is called. Every child is called. We may not know for what, or when, or where. But we are all called to fill a purpose in God's kingdom, and we need to be prepared. We need to know the Scriptures so we know we can depend on God. We need to be ready to stand alone for God, to do hard things, to be courageous. Since we don't know what anyone's calling might entail, we ought to do our best to pour into the next generation, equipping them the best we can . . . which also means that we need to be diligent in equipping ourselves.

How do you intentionally prepare yourself to be ready for whatever God might call you to do?

If you are a grandparent, parent, aunt, older sibling, teacher, coach, volunteer worker, or mentor, how do you intentionally help prepare those coming behind you?

Now let's meet the one who is coming behind Elizabeth.

Read aloud Luke 1:26–37.
Who was Joseph's ancestor?

How did Gabriel describe Mary in the eyes of God?

What would Jesus be called?

How long would His kingdom endure?

How did Gabriel describe how this would happen?

Who did Gabriel suggest Mary go visit?

There is a lot to discover in this angelic encounter as well, but we'll save that for tomorrow. For now, pause and reflect on the peace the angel brought to Mary's troubled heart: The Lord is with you. Do not be afraid.

> The Lord is with you. Yes, you!
> In the waiting.
> In the uncertainty.
> In the disappointment.
> In the loss.
> In the despair.
> In the betrayal.
> In the fear of the future.

And with God, nothing is impossible.

WEEK 1 | DAY 4
LEAPING FOR JOY
LUKE 1:28–56

Well, Gabriel definitely wins the award for the most incredible birth announcement! I find it so interesting that when Mary asked a question for clarification she wasn't scolded the way Zechariah had been. Of course, as we mentioned, part of Zechariah's curse of silence may have served as a blessing in disguise, reminding him that the child with whom he had been entrusted needed to be raised to become a mighty servant of God. Unexplainable events surrounding his birth served this purpose. Zechariah, a priest, immersed in the Scriptures, would naturally have much more understanding of the ways of God than a poor, possibly illiterate teenager from a tiny village in Galilee. Despite her unimpressive background, Mary was a girl of great faith and courage.

Even with these characteristics, she still felt afraid. It's important to reflect on the fact that finding favor with God doesn't always equate to the absence of fear. It usually means He's calling us to the unexplainable, to something impossible apart from His power. To something beyond anything we could think, ask, imagine, or dare hope for in our lives—and that means it's going to be a little scary, and definitely outside our comfort zone or current skill set.

I'd say a virgin birth falls into those categories, wouldn't you? Who could she go to talk to about this? Well, God in His great mercy answers Mary's question . . . Go to your cousin Elizabeth. Talk to her. She will believe you. And when you begin to doubt yourself, Mary, the baby inside Elizabeth's womb will remind you what I have told you.

How did Mary respond to Gabriel in Luke 1:38?

I often wonder why God chose Mary. She probably wasn't educated. She didn't come from a priestly family. She wasn't part of the Jewish aristocracy so Jesus could get the best Hebrew education possible. We aren't told of any particular skills or giftedness she had. All we're told is that she was willing to submit to God's plan for her life, no matter how crazy or out of the box it sounded. Pregnant without being married? By God? People would assume she had committed adultery or been defiled by a Gentile merchant or Roman soldier. She would be a disgrace among her people.

I think the answer is depicted in her willingness to obey: God's will is my will.

Are you willing to surrender to God like that? Do you truly believe in your heart that God's plans for your life are better than anything you have planned for yourself?

Record your thoughts below, maybe writing out a prayer to the Lord where you're struggling . . .

So, off Mary goes to her cousin Elizabeth's house in the hill country of Judea. This was a dangerous trek in those days and would have taken several days to complete. I must say, as a mother of a young teenager, I would be a bit reluctant about allowing my daughter to go, especially if I didn't quite understand the reason why she insisted on going. And if she told me she was going to become pregnant through God's intervention, I certainly would have some concerns.

What did Elizabeth do when Mary arrived?

Write out Luke 1:45:

How encouraged Mary must have felt at this greeting! As she traveled down from Galilee, the reality of her situation surely began to sink in. What would Joseph say? Would he divorce her? Would her parents believe her? Nazareth was a small village, estimated to be anywhere from 500 to 1,500 people—her story would be the talk of the town. Her family would be shamed. Who would believe such a tale?

Mary desperately needed affirmation and encouragement from her older and wiser relative. Because Elizabeth was the wife of a priest, Mary had the opportunity to not only draw on her cousin's wisdom in life's experiences, she also had the opportunity to be encouraged while in the household of Zechariah and Elizabeth. Elizabeth knew full well what it meant to live in shame and reproach among the women in her village, as one who had been barren for so many years. She understood firsthand the pain and rejection Mary would face.

Mary needed to know she wasn't alone in this, humanly speaking. She had Elizabeth, who believed in her, accepted her, and rejoiced with her at the work of God in her life. Oh, how greatly we all need an Elizabeth, don't we?

A mentor.

A confidante.

A co-laborer in ministry, whether it is in our home or elsewhere. Someone who believes in us when we stop believing in ourselves.

Someone who can remind us what God promised in our darkest hours.

Who has been an Elizabeth in your life?

To whom have you been an Elizabeth?

Have you ever asked God to send you an Elizabeth? Or asked Him to allow you to be an Elizabeth for someone else?

And in Elizabeth's joyful response, Mary's troubles melt away. She leaps into praise. I imagine the women hand in hand dancing around the room as Mary sings these words.

Read aloud Luke 1:46–55.
Write out the one or two verses of Mary's song that speak to you most deeply right now. Why do they do so?

The most beautiful thing about her song is that it is nearly entirely comprised of varying Scriptures that she would have been taught since childhood. What we will see as the rest of the story unfolds is how Mary's baby will be born and begin to fulfill each of these things that Mary sings about here.

WHAT IS THIS CHILD GOING TO BE?

LUKE 1:57–80

John is eight days old now. Zechariah's ability to speak has still not returned, but God had His reasons for the delay. No doubt he wondered when his speech would return. Would he have to wait until his son fulfilled the prophecy spoken over him by Gabriel? Zechariah's muteness served as a very visible reminder that God had chosen their son for greatness. He belonged to the Lord, and they must raise him diligently in God's ways and His truth.

Zechariah's muteness points to a bigger sign as well. For four hundred years, there had been no prophecy in Israel. Malachi was the last prophet, and since his time, Israel remained in captivity under the Persians, Greeks, and presently the Romans, receiving no word from the Lord. (For a very short span of time, following the Maccabean revolt against the Hellenistic—Greek—occupiers, Judea was independent as a Jewish state for eighty years.) Israel had also remained in captivity for four hundred years in Egypt until God sent Moses to deliver them. A new type of deliverance was coming. John would prepare the way. The years of silence were over; God was going to speak.

Read aloud Luke 1:57–66.
When was Zechariah's mouth finally opened?

What question were all of the neighbors and people of Judea asking?

We mentioned how John's name means "The Lord is gracious." Throughout the history of Israel, when God mentioned a new name for Himself, He was revealing an aspect of His character, power, or ability, as well as prophesying before His people something He was about to do on their behalf. Names were viewed as prophetic when given to people as well. John needed a new name, not an old family name, because God was ushering in a new thing through him. And what was that new thing? Freedom from the law and a new era of grace. The graciousness of God was soon to be revealed!

Once Zechariah's tongue was loosed, he became filled with the Holy Spirit and prophesied, offering praise up to God!

Read aloud Luke 1:67–79 and circle the things below that God was going to do (hint, it should be all but one of them!):

- Give them ability to serve Him without fear.
- Rescue them from the hand of their enemies
- Remember His covenant He had made with Abraham
- Overthrow the Romans
- Forgive their sins

Wouldn't it be something if the only time our tongues were loosed we gave praise and honor to God? In what circumstances do you find your speech most honoring to God? Write a number from 1 to 10 next to each applicable activity, with 1 being least honoring and 10 being most.

_____ On social media
_____ Having coffee or lunch with a friend
_____ Around your kitchen table with your family
_____ In your small group, Sunday school class, or Bible study
_____ At work or in your classroom
_____ In a private conversation with your spouse/significant other

What do you notice about your speech and your activities? Any patterns? Any changes you'd like to see happen?

Describe John's childhood according to Luke 1:80.

The desert was a place of great symbolism for the Jews. Moses had led the Israelites through the desert to achieve their deliverance. Prophecies from Isaiah 40 about preparing the way of the Lord in the desert were cited by the gospel writers (Matt. 3:3, Mark 1:2–3, John 1:23). Some devout Jews, the Essenes, moved into the desert and dedicated themselves to a greater level of purity in anticipation of His coming. Many of them were scribes, and it is from this group that we have received the Dead Sea Scrolls.

Historically we know the Essenes frequently adopted Jewish orphans. It may be that John's parents passed away before he was fully raised and as a result, he was taken in by the Essenes. We don't know exactly, but we can surmise that Luke is trying to tell us that his upbringing was atypical in some regard.

Similar to how John's life would unfold, the prophecy his father spoke over him tells more about Jesus than it does about John himself. This mighty prophet eagerly and quickly took a back seat to Jesus. He never sought followers for himself, only to point them to Christ. What a beautiful lesson that is for us today! He served as a guide to the Savior.

I love the way the Holy Spirit described the work of Jesus through Zechariah's prophecy. He would bring light, salvation, and peace. Some people insist they don't need "religion" or that all religions are "the same." I dare you to find a savior who offers these three things—light, salvation, and peace—unconditionally. And I double dare you to find a person who does not need at least one of these three things in their life to a greater degree.

What is an area of your life that feels dark to you right now?

That feels dead?

Where there is discord?

Jesus came to bring light, salvation, and peace. To you. No matter who you are or what you have done. No matter if you're the one who willingly brought the darkness, death, and discord into your life or if someone else dragged you into it. He came for you. And His light, salvation, and peace that He offers? Well, let's just say, it's unexplainable.

unexplainable

BIRTH

WEEK 2 | DAY 1
AN UNEXPLAINABLE PEACE
LUKE 2:1–15

Luke is writing a historical narrative, defending both the humanity and deity of Christ. Time and again we will see him reference the prophecies spoken of Christ by the angels, Elizabeth, Mary, Zechariah, and this week two more: Simeon and Anna.

It is important to remember that the prophecies Luke cites in his gospel were steeped in Scriptures, which are now our Old Testament. Luke is not merely showing how Jesus fulfilled that which these people had personally spoken, but rather how Jesus is the fulfillment of all the prophecies throughout the history of Israel. You might suggest that Luke was the original biblical apologist.

He surrounds his defense with indisputable historical facts that could easily be corroborated using extrabiblical sources, adding further weight to the intricacy and exactness of his research and arguments. Remember what the author himself told us as to his purpose in writing: "that you may have certainty concerning the things you have been taught." So, who's ready? Let's start looking at Unexplainable Jesus and discover how very unique He is and the perfect fulfillment of every promise made throughout the ages!

Read aloud Luke 2:1–5.
Who was the emperor of the Roman Empire at this time?

Why did Joseph have to go to Bethlehem?

Who went with him?

Caesar Augustus drastically changed the administration of the Roman Empire. He was the adopted son of Julius Caesar, who was also his great-uncle, and under Julius's reign, civil war had broken out across the empire. Augustus, also known as Octavian, ended the war, secured the empire against its enemies, and became heralded as the "Savior" of Rome. Since the Roman Empire was thought to include the entire world, he was further lauded as "Savior of the World."

Augustus dismantled the Roman Senate, transforming Rome from a republic to a dictatorship. On Augustus's birthday, the empire would celebrate, with Roman choirs singing praise and glory to their great Caesar declaring the "good news" of his reign. This is what Luke is bringing to mind in the opening of this scene.

While a census had not been conducted for some time due to the instability of the empire, Augustus reinstituted the practice. These censuses were not conducted across the entire empire simultaneously; rather, the governors of their provinces would implement them at their preferred time. Some have suggested that Joseph owned property in Bethlehem, which is why he was directed to return to that town. Others stay with the straight reading of the text, that he went to Bethlehem because of his ancestral line. Either way, it was a fulfillment of prophecy (see Micah 5:2).

Women were not required to present themselves at a census, and, in that culture, it's doubtful that Mary ordinarily would have traveled at this stage of her pregnancy. Generally, at this time, especially with a young woman's first birth, a midwife would come and care for her, but in no gospel account is a midwife ever mentioned. Presumably, Joseph alone cared for her.

Within these few short details we see Luke begin to make his first defense. In fact, Luke references the bloodline of David no less than five times in the first two chapters.

Look back at Luke 1:32 and 69. What prophecy regarding Jesus did Joseph help fulfill?

Read the prophecy God gave to David in 2 Samuel 7:12–13. What did God promise him?

What prophecy did God make concerning David in Ezekiel 37:24–28? What occupation did David hold in this prophecy?

In case anyone missed it, Jesus is a descendant of David! The Jews believed that Messiah would be a descendant of David. But He is so much more than that! Let's move on.

Read aloud Luke 2:6–15.
What happened while Mary and Joseph were in Bethlehem?

Who was first told about Jesus' birth?

How did the angel describe this announcement?

How specifically would the shepherds know when they had found the right baby?

What did the angels say would come to men as a result of this child's birth?

What did the shepherds do after the angels returned to heaven?

Jesus, the great shepherd of Israel, the true King of the world, is contrasted with the current king of the world: Caesar Augustus. While we read of shepherding analogies in Scripture and can understand why God used them to illustrate beautiful truths of His care and guidance, it is important to understand that shepherding in biblical times was an occupation of very low status.[1] Isn't it such God's way that He would select the great king of Israel, David, from the sheep fold? Then again choose the King of the World to be revealed to shepherds!

Some scholars suggest that due to Bethlehem's proximity to Jerusalem (under six miles), these shepherds may have had the responsibility of caring for the sheep that were used for sacrifice in the temple. How fitting that the promised Lamb of God would first be revealed to the men who spent their lives caring for the annual Passover Lambs!

Every spring each Jewish family would select a lamb and slaughter it on Passover as a sacrifice for their sins. Jesus became the final sacrifice for sins through His death on the cross.

For more on the Jewish Passover celebration, visit *Come to the Table* at www.ericawiggenhorn.com.

And within this beautiful angelic encounter we see the second mention of Jesus fulfilling prophecy.

How did Gabriel describe the coming events in Luke 1:19?

How did Mary describe God's actions in Luke 1:48?

What did Zechariah prophesy God would provide for His people in Luke 1:79?

Jesus' arrival is the good news of salvation, which brings peace to men.

Peace with God.
Peace among men.
Peace within themselves.

Friend, do you need peace in your life today?

WEEK 2 | DAY 2
A HEART FULL OF TREASURE
LUKE 2:15–35

It really is a shame there were no cellphones and YouTube in those days. Wouldn't it be something if these shepherds could have gone into Jerusalem, whipped out their iPhone and said, "Look! See for yourselves!"? Of course, anyone into photography and graphic design knows you can create just about anything digitally and make it look real. And so it is with the people: some believe their account is true and others think it's fabricated.

What word is used to describe the people's reaction in Luke 2:18?

Who specifically responded in this way?

I can't help but believe part of this "all" included Mary and Joseph. This young man and woman have a heavy weight to bear. Their community no doubt shamed them. We have no reason to believe anyone accepted Mary's claim of an angelic appearance at this point. In their inexperience, poverty, and humanness, they too most likely needed a reminder that God was with them. And with their child.

Write out Luke 2:19:

The term "treasured up" is the Greek word *syntero*.[2] Mary attempted to perpetually keep these things in the forefront of her thoughts. She intensely guarded these memories. We are also told she pondered them, so while she kept the details fresh in her mind, she still did not fully grasp the significance of all that was happening.

I cannot help but contrast Mary's reaction to all of this with how the shepherds reacted.

What did the shepherds do in Luke 2:20?

Herein lies the difference. The shepherds only witnessed the wonderful. Mary had become wounded while carrying the wonderful. She had faced fears. Had nearly been rejected by her betrothed. Given birth alone. No offense to Joseph, but I doubt he was all that helpful. The shepherds would've probably known more of what to do birthing sheep in the fields. Not much cross-over in carpentry and childbirth.

Mary, no doubt, had a thousand questions and a million emotions swirling through her young heart and mind. And God, in His tender mercy, would continue to offer her affirmation and prepare her for what lay ahead. And He will do the same for us. Together we will treasure and ponder who this Unexplainable Jesus is and in the midst of a life that often wounds us, may we discover the wonder of all that He is.

Mary has done a lot of traveling since her initial angelic encounter with Gabriel. She went down to Judea to stay with her cousin Elizabeth, and then she returned home. She traveled down to Judea a second time with Joseph to register for the census in Bethlehem. She will now travel a third time, in this case, to the holy city of Jerusalem, to fulfill her vows to the Lord for the birth of her son. Matthew tells us that at some point, Mary and Joseph again traveled all the way to Egypt where they would remain until it was safe to return home (see Matt. 2:13–16). As their trip to Bethlehem would remain forever etched within Mary's heart, so now would their trip to Jerusalem.

Read aloud Luke 2:22–24.

According to Exodus 13:1–2 and 14–16, for what reason did God command the Israelites to offer a sacrifice for their firstborn son?

Mary and Joseph were devout followers of Judaism. They followed the law of circumcision and also the command to dedicate their firstborn son to the Lord. They had been obedient to the command Gabriel had given Mary and named Jesus as he had said. Jesus means "The Lord is salvation" and indeed this tiny baby, God in the flesh, had been born to become the salvation of the world.

Read aloud Luke 2:25–32.
How is Simeon described?

For what was Simeon eagerly waiting?

What had God promised him?

How did Simeon describe Jesus in vv. 30–32?

Oh, to be a Simeon! To pray for the salvation of the world over our own personal needs! To be troubled in spirit until you see the salvation of souls brought from darkness to light! Think of the expectancy in which he lived—prayerfully searching for the coming Messiah. I'd love to say I lived in such a prayerful state of mind, but I can't. Most of my prayers reflect my personal needs and desires, and

I am often more troubled in spirit over my own disappointments and inconveniences than I am over the eternal state of a stranger's soul. How does one develop a heart like Simeon—who cares more about the salvation of others than he does about himself?

How does Simeon's prophecy over Jesus compare with Zechariah's in Luke 1:68–71? Namely, who else does Simeon include in the salvation plan?

What did Isaiah say about this group of people according to Isaiah 42:6 and 49:6?

It is important to note that the concept of Gentile inclusion in God's salvation plan was not strictly a New Testament concept. The Jewish people understood that God offered His salvation to the Gentiles all along. But they thought you had to convert to Judaism in order to receive it, or follow the law of Moses. In these verses, our eyes are opened to the fact that salvation for Gentiles, indeed all salvation, would not come through the law of Moses, but rather through this tiny infant who would grow to become our ultimate sacrifice for sin.

Read aloud Luke 2:33–35.
How do Mary and Joseph respond to Simeon's words?

What dark prophecy did Simeon now speak over Jesus?

Could their son really be the Messiah? To say they marveled meant they considered such a possibility to be nothing short of miraculous. I find it so interesting that the dark portion of the prophecy is given to Mary only. Joseph is not included. Only she would witness Him being spoken against and have her heart pierced with sorrow.

We cannot know for sure, but it appears Joseph was absent during Jesus' adult life. After age twelve, we have no biblical record of Joseph being present. We do not know what happened to him, but Mary would face the ultimate rejection of her son without her husband by her side.

Can you imagine what Mary may have been feeling in this moment? Simeon said her soul would be pierced. Meaning she, along with her son, would suffer. Can you imagine holding a tiny infant in your arms and someone coming along telling you that He is going to suffer? As a mother, I don't think there is anything much harder in this life than having to watch your children suffer. I would hands down choose my own suffering over my children's any day of the week. As Mary clutched her tiny baby in her arms, a stab of fear must have punctured her heart knowing the road ahead would not be an easy one.

As you contemplate your own road ahead, craft your own prayer to God below:

WEEK 2 | DAY 3
ANOTHER WITNESS
LUKE 2:36–40

When someone tells me something incredulous about another person, besides considering the validity of the source, I often take it lightly. However, when I hear the same thing twice, both from credible sources, I tend to believe there might be some truth to the tale. In Jewish thought, court cases needed the presence of at least two witnesses in order to be valid.[3] How fitting that we are told of not one, but two righteous persons asserting that the baby Jesus is the Messiah who was to come.

Read aloud Luke 2:36–38.
What credentials are given to Anna that her words should hold weight?

Based on her actions, how certain do you think she was that Jesus was the Messiah?

Anna went and told "all who were waiting" with her (see Luke 2:38). She spilled the beans in her prayer circle. I have to admit, I'm a bit envious of Anna. What would it be like to recognize Jesus so readily? It would be one thing to recognize Jesus' authority when you watched Him cast out demons or calm a storm, but here was a baby lying in His mother's arms, and Anna recognized Him as the expected one! How did the Holy Spirit reveal it to her?

I think I often go through life missing Jesus. Unless He is doing something big, I fail to recognize Him. I'm in too much of a hurry to notice the whisper of the Holy Spirit in my heart prompting me to approach the stranger right in front of me. It's easy to see Jesus in the extraordinary, but in my everyday worship fulfilling my everyday duty, my gaze can move right past Him. And it's often in the simple that Jesus does the spectacular.

Describe a time when you witnessed Jesus at work in simple, everyday life:

Describe a time when you know Jesus worked through you while you were going about your regular day:

After extraordinary encounters in Jerusalem, Jesus is going back home to an everyday life in the small village of Nazareth. We have already discussed that some portion of His childhood was spent in Egypt, but we are not explicitly told when this occurred. Did Mary and Joseph share with their family and friends the extraordinary things that had happened in Bethlehem and Jerusalem, or did they keep them to themselves? We just do not know and can only speculate beyond what Scripture tells us. Next, we get a glimpse of Jesus as a youth.

Read aloud Luke 2:40.

What three things did Jesus possess in His youth?

I love how Luke describes Mary and Joseph by saying, "they performed everything" according to the law of the Lord (see Luke 2:39). We saw in Mary's song with Elizabeth that she was a young woman versed in the Scriptures. This young couple took their role as Jewish parents seriously, training their son in the sacred texts. The coupling of God's grace on Him with the faithful teaching of His parents resulted in a young man ready to dialogue with some of Israel's most elite teachers in Jerusalem.

Have you had someone in your life who was committed to training you in the Scriptures? How did that impact your life?

Whose life could you impact by sharing Scripture with them?

WEEK 2 | DAY 4
MY FATHER'S HOUSE
LUKE 2:41-52

My daughter is getting ready to turn fourteen in a few months. Life with her is hysterical giggles one minute and solemn contemplation the next. She seems to vacillate between childhood and adulthood faster than the wind shifts. Sometimes, something will come out of her mouth so profound, I am in awe at her wisdom. Such is life with a young teen.

We are only given one small snapshot into Jesus' childhood, and it is when He was about the age my daughter is now. Maybe that's why the event strikes me so deeply. Here we see the very beginning of Jesus becoming a man.

Read aloud Luke 2:41–44.
How often did Mary and Joseph travel to Jerusalem for the Passover Feast?

What happened after the feast was over?

There were three pilgrimage feasts in Jewish life: the Passover Feast, Pentecost, and the Feast of Ingathering. The Law required the Jewish people to come to Jerusalem three times per year for these feasts. In Jesus' day, most devout Jews living in Israel would come to all three feasts, but if they could only attend one, it was generally Passover.

This was the largest of all pilgrimage feasts and Jews from all over the known world would converge upon the city. Villagers traditionally caravanned to and from the city in large groups, protecting them from bandits along the road. Such appears to be the case with Mary and Joseph, and they assumed Jesus was somewhere within their large traveling party.

Read aloud Luke 2:45–50.

How long did it take to find Jesus once they discovered He was missing?

Where did they finally locate Him, and what was He doing?

How did those around Him respond to His questions and answers?

How did His parents feel when they witnessed Jesus conversing in the temple?

What did Mary say to Him?

How did He answer her?

I wish I could think of a modern-day analogy to paint the picture as to what is happening here. Imagine an inner-city child, or maybe someone who had barely been schooled, sitting on the steps of a seminary asking the theology professors profound questions and responding back to their statements with unmistakably wise answers. What would these highly educated theologians think of this?

What would this child's parents think? How would they feel stepping into such a circle of intellect?

Mary, no doubt with a mixture of relief and frustration, wants to know why Jesus had not stayed with them as He should have. Jesus' answer is both profound and innocent at the same time. In His youth, He seems to have no thought of the dangers that could have occurred to leave a young boy in a large, crowded city flooded with travelers. Yet His answer also reflects a deep awareness of His identity and mission. God is His Father. And He should be where His Father is and doing what His Father would have Him be doing, namely learning the Scriptures. He also seems to believe that this is exactly where Mary and Joseph would have Him to be.

I believe Mary and Joseph had been extremely diligent in teaching Him in light of all of the wonders surrounding His birth. Into the fully human yet fully divine young man, wisdom of the Scriptures had been faithfully imparted along with a love for God and a zeal for His holy temple. And while Jesus sat within its walls, the tension mounted between the innocence of childhood and the wisdom of adulthood. While Jesus appears to be fully aware of who He was, His parents still did not fully understand.

Read aloud Luke 2:51–52.

Once they arrived back in Nazareth, how did Mary process all that had happened?

Describe how Jesus was viewed during His teen years.

While Jesus obviously could have become the next rabbinic student, dialoguing with the best of them, He instead returned home to His small village in Nazareth, learning carpentry from His father, Joseph. How beautiful that God in the flesh made His dwelling among the craftsman instead of the religious elite. In the sheep pens and the wheat fields, Jesus experienced the glory of God, not the grandeur of the temple. The Savior of the world made His home among the poor, downcast, and the needy, waiting for the will of His Father to reveal to Him the time to no longer conceal His glory.

Jesus spent most of His life in the ordinary streets and homes of ordinary people. He met God in the solitude of the grassy hills and felt His peace on the lull of the sea. One of the most unexplainable things about Jesus is that we can always find Him in the midst of the everyday. Suddenly, He is there. In the most unexpected and regular of places. And with His presence comes an unexplainable peace. Maybe before you close your study book today, you'd like to pause and ask Jesus to reveal Himself to you in your everyday, ordinary life. Ask Him for eyes to see Him right where you are.

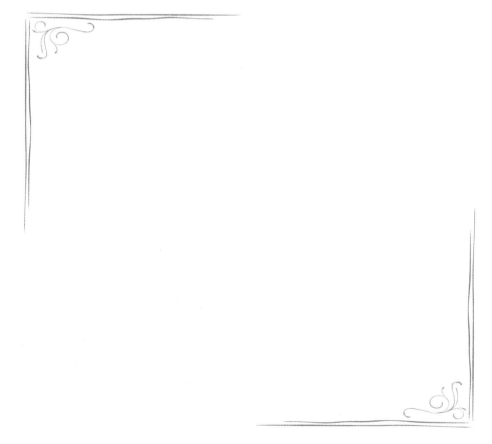

THE ONE WHO IS TO COME

LUKE 3:1–38

Within these everyday scenes of dust and dirt along Galilee's shores, Luke opens the heavens and drops down the glorious, bringing the human and divine into harmony in the person of unexplainable Jesus. He insists that Jesus will fulfill the long-awaited prophecies of Isaiah—making the path to salvation easy and accessible for all.

According to Luke 3:3, what was John the Baptist's primary message?

Based on your reading of Luke 3:4–10, would you describe John's message as comforting or confrontational?

What question did the people ask in response to his message?

Judaism was a works-based theology. Therefore, if they really repented, it precipitated action and thus their question to John.

Read aloud Luke 3:10–14. Complete the following chart, listing John's expected demonstration of true repentance:

WHO	WHAT THEY WERE TO DO
The general crowd	
The tax collectors	
The soldiers	

I could easily translate these actions into abstract attitudes: generous, honest, humble, and content. Interestingly, all John's exhortations center around money and tangibles. Let's pause here for a moment.

How does our abundance or our lack influence our generosity?

How might our desire for certain things create temptation to be dishonest?

How might money or possessions, or even lack of them, lure us into pride?

What would it look like to truly be content with what we currently have?

A common belief at the time was that the coming of Messiah was linked to Israel's repentance. John's call to repentance is messianic language. Luke portrays for us the extent of John's ministry by including these tax collectors and soldiers. They were the biggest sinners of the lot of Israel—both considered sellouts to Rome and no longer true Jews. Some scholars believe these soldiers may not have even been Jews at all, but Roman mercenaries.

Since John's revival toward repentance spread like wildfire, many wondered if he might be the Messiah. He immediately squelched any such thoughts.

Read Luke 3:15–20.
How does John describe the one who was to come?

Will He come as a comforter or a confronter?

Why do you think Luke describes this as "good news"?

The terrors of Rome could not compare to the sins of Israel in the hearts and minds of the people. Have you ever sat through a sermon and felt the urge to nudge the person next to you thinking, "This word is so meant for you—I sure hope you're listening!" never thinking for a second as to how the admonition might apply to your own thoughts, habits, or choices?

The advent of Messiah, believed the Jews of that time, meant the liberation of Israel, with no foreign oppression, no injustice, and peace and prosperity. They eagerly welcomed unquenchable fire on the Romans and on Herod, their puppet king. This was the best news they'd heard all day. Just tell us what to do, John! We are eager for the Messiah to arrive! In the midst of this expectation, however, Jesus enters, humble and meek, submitted to the will of God.

Read Luke 3:21–23.
What event is happening here and how does God respond to it?

I often wondered why Jesus needed to be baptized if He were sinless. While Jesus Himself was sinless, He knew that His mission was to take on all of the sins of the world. Jesus repented on behalf of all the sinful people He would save. Rather than the attitude of Israel to look around at the person next to them and say, "I sure hope they are hearing this message," Jesus humbly came submitted to the will of His Father to become the sacrifice for our sins.

The baptism of Jesus was a sign of obedience to His Father to fulfill His mission as the Savior of the world. Israel's mission—and subsequently ours today—was to repent of our sinfulness and believe we need Jesus' saving grace to become the righteousness of God to a world desperate for hope. Do we look around in search of others who appear more sinful than ourselves, or do we humbly submit ourselves to the cleansing power of Christ in desperation?

unexplainable
INTRODUCTIONS

ANCIENT PROMISES FULFILLED

LUKE 4:14–44

Throughout human history we see one of two things occur when someone famous returns to their hometown: they are either highly venerated or despised. Jesus experienced both responses within the course of one sermon in His hometown of Nazareth. In Luke's gospel, we have not been specifically informed of any miracles done by Jesus as of yet. But when we piece Luke's story chronologically with the other three gospel accounts, we know that Jesus' return to Nazareth comes after He has been teaching elsewhere for a while, and also after He turns the water into wine in Cana (see John 2:1–12).

Remember, Nazareth is a small village numbering about five hundred people, meaning everybody there knows Jesus and He knows them.[4] He has developed quite the reputation as a teacher at this point, so it makes sense that He would be asked to expound on the Scriptures during a synagogue service.

Read aloud Luke 4:14–21.

Typically, in one of these services several prayers were recited, then a portion from the Law—the first five books in our Bibles—and finally a section from the prophets would be read. These Scriptures were written on scrolls in Hebrew. After being read, they would be verbally paraphrased into the common language of Aramaic and an exposition would be offered as to their meaning and application. A synagogue ruler would often choose the portions of Scripture to be read and assign them to the teacher. Luke intimates that Jesus was handed the scroll of the prophet Isaiah, but He personally selected the portion of the prophecy to be read, because in most cases they would read closer to twenty-one verses at a time, and Jesus quotes only Isaiah 61:1 and the first part of verse 2.[5] Don't be confused by the slight differentiation in wording. Isaiah 61 has been translated into English from Hebrew and Luke's gospel has been translated into English from Greek. For this reason we see the exact same idea, with slightly different wording.

Write Isaiah 61:2 below and circle the part Jesus removes from His reading:

It is no wonder the eyes of all in the synagogue were on Him—they would have been stunned at the abruptness of His reading, wondering why He had ended so suddenly. Can you imagine if your pastor stood up to preach on Sunday morning, uttered one sentence and then just stood there, staring at you? Awkward! What Jesus did next shocked them even more.

What did Jesus claim in Luke 4:21?

Not one person in that synagogue had any doubt about what Jesus was implying. Isaiah's prophecy referred to the coming of the Messiah. And Jesus just said the Messiah was among them—today. But Jesus also said something else by omitting the rest of the text. He wasn't bringing vengeance—He was bringing grace. And now comes the divergent response.

The people in the crowd spoke two things in response to Jesus' claim.

- They spoke well of Him and the graciousness of His words.
- They refused to believe that the boy they knew as Joseph's son could possibly be the Messiah.

Their question is not one of joyous surprise, but rather contempt. "We know you, Jesus. We know your history. And you want us to believe you are the Messiah?! Please!" So Jesus responds to their unbelief.

Read aloud Luke 4:23–30.
What did Jesus claim the people would say to Him?

Could it be that Jesus knew their hearts and why they had flooded into that little synagogue to hear Him? They were hoping to witness a miracle.

Interestingly, the same temptations that Jesus faced in the wilderness are again presented here in His hometown of Nazareth. He could perform a miracle before them to prove His authority. He could call on His Father to confirm His identity. He could abandon His mission because establishing an earthly kingdom would not require paying sin's penalty. Or He could continue in submission to the will of His Father. Just like the followers of John the Baptist, the folks at Nazareth wanted a Messiah who would bring vengeance on their enemies.

What two prophets does Jesus quote, and whom did they help?

During Elijah's time, the king of Israel, Ahab, was married to the Sidonian princess, Jezebel. After the marriage, Jezebel began killing off the Lord's prophets and made the worship of God illegal in the nation of Israel. The Sidonians were Israel's enemies, and Jezebel represented the height of pagan wickedness. Zarephath was a famous town in Sidon.

During Elisha's time, the Syrians were Israel's chief opponents, continually raiding and destroying the nation of Israel. Yet God in His mercy sent His mighty prophets to aid these wicked people. Elisha healed Naaman, the Syrian king's highest commander, from his leprosy. Jesus' audience is putting the pieces together and they are furious. Not only is Jesus claiming to be the Messiah and bringing grace rather than vengeance, but He is suggesting that He will bring grace to the vilest of Israel's enemies.

What did the people desire to do to Jesus after hearing His sermon?

In the midst of this painful rejection, God provides miraculous protection. Jesus escapes from His hometown unharmed physically, though one can scarcely imagine the scars in His soul after facing the scorn of those who, for His entire life, had comprised His home and community. Can you imagine responding in such anger to the next-door neighbor you grew up with that you wanted to kill him in cold blood? Completely and utterly alone, except for the presence of His Father, Jesus returns to Capernaum to gather a new family around Him.

When Jesus arrives in Capernaum, He receives a different kind of welcome.

Read aloud Luke 4:31–37.
Who was the first to recognize Jesus' identity and authority?

Over and over in his narrative thus far, Luke emphasizes Jesus' identity (human and divine), His authority over all things and His mission.

What does the unclean spirit's question to Jesus imply about his understanding of who Jesus is and what is His mission?

I believe this is one of the reasons why our enemy works so hard to confuse us about our identity in Christ and our authority over the power of darkness. The enemy is not omniscient and, while he has been a student of God and humanity for thousands of years, he does not know how mightily God could use you or me in His rescue mission of the world. He trembles at the thought of it.

Rather than allowing us to find out or having to witness it himself, the enemy works hard to divert and distract us from God's plan. He tempts us to establish our own identity and assert our authority rather than rest in God's ability to do so on our behalf, just as he tempted Christ. Until we begin to fully embrace submission to God, the enemy will effectively keep us from our mission.

Jesus became stripped of His earthly identity in order to fulfill His heavenly mission. He was misunderstood by His immediate family as well as his hometown community, and was called to create a new community and family with His followers. The Son of God. His identity and authority rested in God alone. And God would fulfill His mission in and through Him.

Maybe you can relate. Maybe your family has even rejected you. You prefer to stay away from where you grew up. You've been painfully labeled by your past. As a follower of Jesus, you have a new identity—child of God. And as a result, you hold a new authority, Jesus' authority to speak life and healing over the wounds others have inflicted. And God has a plan to fulfill in and through you as well.

What are some earthly titles by which you are identified?

What type of significance, authority, or pain do those titles bring you?

How could clinging too tightly to those titles possibly prevent you from fulfilling God's mission for your life?

If we have decided to follow Jesus, our life is now hidden with Christ in God (see Colossians 3:3). We have a new identity. We have authority over the powers of darkness that seek and scheme to keep us held captive. And we have a mission to become colaborers in God's kingdom, producing the most glorious results the world has ever seen, bringing satisfaction and significance beyond our wildest dreams. Take a good look in the mirror today, dear one. You are a child of the King.

SOMETHING FROM NOTHING
LUKE 5:1–26

Jesus leaves Nazareth after a painful rejection from his hometown and arrives in Capernaum. Here the powers of darkness keenly announce His new identity and authority. Luke also reminds us in these next few scenes of Jesus' mission.

Look back at Luke 4:18–19, 38–41.

How would the miracles Jesus has performed thus far in Luke's gospel affirm that Jesus has already begun fulfilling His mission He had quoted in Isaiah?

All around the Sea of Galilee there is a zig-zagging coastline, forming lots of natural inlets, with the land sloping downward toward the seashore. Geographically each inlet creates its own amphitheater in which several thousand people could easily gather. Within the inlet, even a person speaking in a normal voice could be heard throughout, as the sound waves naturally reverberate across the u-shaped hill in front of the sea.

> For a photo of this scene, visit *Come to the Table*
> at www.ericawiggenhorn.com.

From here, Jesus spoke to the crowds. Because of what Jesus does next, we can presume Simon Peter is in the boat.

Why is Simon Peter reluctant to follow Jesus' instruction?

What happens when he finally concedes?

How does Simon respond to this miracle?

I want to put ourselves in Simon's shoes or, shall we say, sit on his boat for a moment. These professional fishermen in Galilee knew you caught fish at night. No one in their right mind tries to catch fish in the middle of the day in the Sea of Galilee. It's a waste of time. I don't think Peter expected a miracle. He certainly didn't respond like someone who had just witnessed Jesus do what he had been anticipating all along.

It got me thinking. What if Peter's *nothing* was so that Jesus could come along and do *something*? What if our effort, resulting in *nothing*, was Jesus' plan to show up and do *something unexplainable*?

Have you ever had a circumstance, situation, or relationship in your life where you felt like you were laboring your heart out with little to no results?

What kind of hope would it bring you to realize that your nothing was so that Jesus could come and do something unexplainable?

That was certainly what Jesus did in Peter's, Andrew's, James's, and John's situations. With little to no detail, these four men up and left all they had ever known and embarked on a new adventure: fishing for men. Jesus was asking them to forsake their current life and community of daily fishing and net-making on the

Sea of Galilee, to travel with Jesus throughout Israel as He taught and performed miracles. Together, they would establish a new community: the year of the Lord's favor, also known as the kingdom of God.

Read aloud Luke 5:12–16 and discover the first man they see Jesus restore to community.

How would you describe this man's faith in Jesus' power and authority?

Jesus spoke to the man, but He did something even more profound. What was it?

What did Jesus tell the man to do after He healed him with His touch?

I'm not sure you or I can fully comprehend the tenderness of this moment. In Jesus' day when there was no modern medicine, disease containment was all a society could do to prevent its spread of infection. Therefore, lepers were outcasts. Due to the extent of his leprosy, it is quite possible that this man had not felt the physical touch of another human being for years or possibly decades.

Think of the loneliness. This desperate leper wanted more than release from his disease, he wanted restoration back into community. And Jesus gave that to him. Once he went to the priest and he was declared clean, he could renew the relationships that had been torn from him. I find this scene so beautiful in light of Jesus' own isolation and rejection from His family, friends, and neighbors. Jesus understood just how deeply this man craved a touch of acceptance and affection. Jesus was seldom alone, and yet I believe He knew the deep pain of loneliness.

Read Luke 4:42, 5:16.

Whom did Jesus seek to satisfy His deep desire for belonging?

To whom did Jesus go, and from whom did He disengage, in order to be replenished physically, emotionally, and spiritually?

We were created for community. Have you ever felt left out? Or as though you were somehow different from everyone else and just didn't quite fit with the rest of the group? I know I have. It can breed feelings of resentment, frustration, and deep insecurity within us. Can you imagine how Jesus must have felt? He literally is different from everyone else and doesn't fit in with the rest of the group. There's no one else on planet Earth who is both human and divine at the same time. He is completely alone in this identity. Even the Father is somewhat separated from His experience. And yet, He and the Father are one. It's mind-boggling, really. No wonder Jesus so deeply craved community with the Father while clothed in human flesh.

Read aloud Luke 5:17–26 and experience the beauty of community.

What kind of man do you think this paralytic was that his friends went to such great lengths to bring him to Jesus?

Do you have friends like that in your life?

Have you ever been that kind of friend to someone else?

Let's pause for a moment and imagine what the church would look like to the world if we became people who exhibited those types of friendships—people who would do just about anything to bring their friends to the feet of Jesus—mat-carrying, roof-raising, believing-the-best-for-you kind of friends!

Can you imagine standing there in the midst of Jesus' teaching and all of a sudden there is a bunch of commotion above you and then you see men lowering some guy down on a mat in front of Jesus? There was a big crowd of people there. And many of them were important people: scribes, Pharisees, and teachers of the Law. You didn't tear apart the top of someone's house and interrupt people like that. These friends have got some guts! These guys know that if they can get their friend in front of Jesus, miracles can happen.

What does Jesus say to the man before Him?

How do the scribes and Pharisees respond to this?

It seems strange that Jesus tells the man his sins are forgiven. To the religious leaders this amounted to blasphemy, as only God could forgive another man's sin. Jesus is challenging their long-held traditions that illness and demonic possession were due to sin: either the person's directly or their parents' (see John 9:1–2). Essentially Jesus poses this question: "If illness is indeed from sin, and I can heal illnesses, then shouldn't you naturally conclude that I have power over sin?" He is backing them into a corner. If Jesus can forgive sins, that means He is God, because only God can forgive sins. He is creating tension here that can only be resolved in one of two ways:

Either illness isn't really from sin and therefore how these religious leaders viewed sick people was not true

or

Jesus was God in human flesh since He had the power to heal diseases.

The religious leaders did not like either of these options. To what conclusion is Jesus hoping they will arrive? I believe it is that they will see their own sinfulness. It would not matter if they believed He was God if they never acknowledged their own sinfulness. Even the demons acknowledged His deity. It was their admission of their own desperation that Jesus was after.

And herein lies the secret to becoming the kind of church I invited us all to imagine above. When we become people who readily admit our own desperation for Jesus, the door opens—or the roof is dismantled—for us to become people who will do anything to bring our friends to the feet of Jesus as well as to have their sins forgiven. When we remember that we once were helpless on a mat until someone else brought us to Jesus, we become willing to carry someone else to His feet in hopeful expectation.

Read aloud Luke 5:26 and notice the people's response.

I don't think the people were in awe just because the man walked. Luke already told us that Jesus had been performing many miracles. This was yet another one of them. I think it was the entire scene in which the miracle unfolded that left them in awe. The people whom they had been taught to revere as holy and wise, the Pharisees and teachers of the Law, were the people Jesus had openly challenged (see especially v. 22). A lame man, for reasons unbeknownst to any of them, had been so tangibly served and loved by friends in the most unselfish of ways. Most of the people who witnessed this miracle would have judged him, assuming his paralytic condition represented God's judgment on him. Jesus had been moved by the faith and audacity of his friends. The whole scene was too much to take in. Jesus was turning everything they understood about holiness and sin upside down. What did it all mean?

Guess what, friend? Jesus is still turning everything our friends and neighbors understand about goodness and evil upside down today. Are you and I ready to become mat-carrying, roof-raising, believing-the-best-for-others kind of people? Will we allow Jesus to make us people with such faith and audacity that the world is left in wonder?

A NEW TEACHING

LUKE 5:27–6:11

Luke has told us that Jesus performed many, many miracles, but he chooses to highlight three in particular: the miraculous catch of fish, the healing of the paralytic, and another we will read about today.

Why does he do that? In the first miracle, Luke is demonstrating Jesus' power over nature. In the healing of the paralytic, Jesus demonstrates His power over sickness and disease. In the last of the three, Jesus boldly states that He is Lord of the Sabbath. Luke has carefully highlighted three significant incidents to present Jesus as superior to other faith healers. There were Jewish legends of rabbis being given power to heal people, or supplicate God for healing on their behalf. There were also stories of those afflicted by demonic forces being delivered. Jesus, however, takes the power to heal and perform miracles to a whole new level. Luke intentionally points us to His power over realms of creation thought only to be under the control of God.

So, Luke points out how Jesus is Lord over creation or nature by bringing a miraculous catch of fish; Lord over sin and judgment by removing diseases, such as paralysis, which were sometimes believed to be signs of judgment; and now we are going to see Jesus exercising miraculous power on the Sabbath. In other words, Jesus' power and authority extend to all aspects of human existence.

I'm not sure we can fully wrap our minds around these claims of Jesus. After all, hindsight is always 20/20, and many of us making our way through this study may have already been taught the concept of Jesus' deity. But for the Jews standing before Him as they witnessed these miracles and He made these claims, their minds were spinning.

If a thirty-year-old man stood before us today and told us he was God, we would think he was crazy. If he told us he was God and then started doing things that only God can do like eradicate cancer, miraculously remove addiction, bring drug lords to repentance, and feed an entire city using only one Happy Meal, we'd sit back and try to make sense of it all.

Read aloud Luke 5:27–32.
In this passage, who begins to follow Jesus?

What did he do to celebrate?

Who did the Pharisees complain to specifically?

Who answered their complaints, and what did He say?

I love Jesus' answer here—and His protection over His disciples—stepping in and answering these accusations against them. I wonder if they even picked up on His irony. These "righteous" ones didn't need Jesus' kind of banquet. They were already good to go, at least in their opinion of themselves. Yet again, Jesus invites them to pause and look within their hearts. Their very questioning demonstrates a critical and judgmental spirit.

Read aloud Luke 5:33–39.
To what other group (whom they also didn't like) do the Pharisees compare Jesus and His disciples?

What question does Jesus ask them in return?

Jesus starts using wedding illustrations here. Wine was served at weddings and new garments were worn. What in the world does a wedding have to do with Levi throwing a party for all of his social outcast friends? A wedding symbolized a covenant: God coming into the presence of the bride and groom as they became one. Could it be that Jesus is emphasizing that His presence brings about a time when both the "righteous" and the sinful will enjoy community with each other as never before?

A bride would never tear off a piece of her brand-new wedding dress and sew it onto her grandmother's old, dusty dress that smelled like moth balls and walk down the aisle. Likewise, a catering company isn't going to ditch their fine crystal pitchers and choose to replace them with hot pink plastic ones from the dollar store. That would be ridiculous, unless the crystal is cracked and can no longer hold drinks without leaking all over the guests. Even though the new ones are prettier, as old wineskins produced better and richer flavor than the new, eventually they had to be replaced. And the new ones never seemed to produce the same tasty results as the old ones had. Jesus is illustrating two important points about the arrival of His presence:

- Something new is happening here. It is so brand new, it is going to require a new way of thinking about things. It's radical and won't immediately make sense. If you cannot open your heart and your mind to Him, you'll stick with what you already know and believe, and you'll miss it.

- The "righteous" were comfortable with the status quo. The old system of the Law suited them just fine. They didn't want anything new or radical. Jesus is telling them up front that they will reject Him and the new community of the kingdom His presence will bring.

And with this tension in the forefront of our minds, we are ready to dive into Luke's third miracle, demonstrating that Jesus holds authority over the Sabbath.

Read aloud Luke 6:1–5.
What question did the Pharisees ask Jesus?

What question did Jesus ask in return?

What conclusion did Jesus reach?

Why did Jesus refer to David eating bread? Have you picked up on the fact that Jesus intentionally tells stories that evoke certain emotions, traditions, and long-held beliefs in the hearts of His hearers? David was the most loved and revered king in Israel's history. This story takes place in 1 Samuel 21 when David has to flee Jerusalem because Saul is trying to kill him. There are some striking parallels in the two events.

Saul is trying to destroy David, just as the Pharisees want to destroy Jesus. David is the rightful king, but Saul has yet to be overthrown so he can take his rightful place on the throne. Jesus also is the rightful king of the world, but the current political system still remains in power. David and his followers are constantly being pursued by their enemies just as these Pharisees are consistently trying to trap Jesus. The priest who gives David the bread is unaware of David's mission, just as the Pharisees have yet to grasp the mission of Jesus. David is not deemed sinful in eating the bread of Presence in this account, so why should Jesus be accused of being sinful now?

Lastly, the Jews believed that the Messiah would be a descendant of David who would rule and reign forever. Some scholars suggest that they believed it would literally be David resurrected and reseated on the throne. When Jesus compares Himself to David, He is making a huge claim about Himself. And while they are reeling from the audacity of His comparing Himself to David, He follows it up with an even more brazen statement: He has authority over the Sabbath.

Yahweh instituted the Sabbath at creation, and no one held authority over it but Yahweh alone. Who would dare say such a thing? Luke is going to demonstrate why Jesus could make such a claim in the event he tells us about next.

Read aloud Luke 6:6–11.

Where is Jesus, and what is He doing in verse 6?

What day of the week is it?

Why were the Pharisees and teachers of the Law there?

What question did Jesus pose to the crowd?

How did the Pharisees respond to this miracle?

When we read about "the Law" throughout Scripture, we cannot merely think about our first five books of the Bible, or what the Jews referred to as Torah. The Jews also had an oral law that had been passed down from generation to generation. Much of this is referred to as tradition, but they believed that Moses had received this oral law from God on Mount Sinai at the same time he received the written law, or the Torah. This oral law comprises the Jewish Mishnah along with centuries of exposition on this oral law and new traditions added over time.

By the time Jesus entered the scene, these teachers of the Law had begun to elevate the oral law and their traditions over the simplicity of the written law recorded by Moses. Hundreds of rules had been added, many of which referred to all of the "do nots" on the Sabbath. They had taken God's command not to work on the Sabbath and developed countless applications from it—one of which was that healing should not occur on a Sabbath day.

Now along comes Jesus asking them to look beyond the letter of the law and to examine the intent of the law. What was the intent of the Sabbath? Should it be used as an excuse not to address a striking human need right before their eyes? Would it have been holy to have allowed David and his men to go hungry rather than offering them bread? The purpose of the Sabbath was to rest in the goodness and provision of God. It was a reminder that God alone saved their lives by His saving mercy. Hence the poignancy of Jesus' question: Is it better to do good and to save life?

I'm going to throw out a couple of punches myself today—ones of which I've felt the blow against my own heart and mind first.

Have I gotten to a place where I prefer the old wineskins rather than the new? You know, comfortable, predictable Christianity—where I step into the synagogue (modern-day church) and know what to expect, what's expected of me, and how to neatly tuck it in my own little box of my rules of life I've set up for myself?

Or am I ready for something new? Something radical and unexplainable? Something that is going to infuse new life and flavor?

Let's pause for a moment and invite Jesus into an honest examination of our heart. Respond how you sense Him speaking to you below.

WEEK 3 | DAY 4
EXPECT THE UNEXPECTED
LUKE 6:12–49

We are only a quarter of the way into Luke's gospel and we see that Jesus has already become a highly controversial figure. The teachers of the Law understand very clearly the claims Jesus is making, and while His power and authority remain unexplainable apart from the work of God, they are unwilling to accept Him.

I often hear people ask, "Why is it that those who most diligently studied the prophecies regarding Messiah were unable to recognize Jesus when He arrived?" I think a careful reading of Jesus' interactions with them provides a clear and compelling answer: they were unwilling to admit their own sinfulness. They were blinded by their pride. To accept Jesus meant they had to accept His teaching that they could not save themselves.

According to Jesus, these men were as sinful as the tax collector, prostitute, and pagan. But according to the people of Israel, the Pharisees and teachers of the Law were holy and revered. It takes a tremendous amount of humility to give up your status, renown, and position and come as a beggar at the feet of Jesus.

Read aloud Luke 6:12–16.
What important decision did Jesus make, and what did He do before making it?

I certainly don't need to hammer home the importance of prayer before decision-making. But I do want us to understand the significance of the decision made. What did it mean exactly when Jesus called them His "apostles"? Consider the following explanation:

The rabbis used the word primarily in contexts that are neither explicitly theological nor religious but rather have to do with matters of the Law. The word is used of individuals who are "temporarily authorized to carry fully in their own person the person and rights of another in the accomplishment of some act." The oft-cited passage from the Mishna provides a clear definition: "The one who is sent (shaliach) is the same as the one who sends." The basis for such a practice lay in the Old Testament law of the messenger, where the reaction paid to messengers is at the same time paid to the one who sent them.[6]

These twelve men now hold an authority that the other disciples do not receive from Jesus.

Consider this additional explanation of the term "apostle":

The Hebrew verb underlying this description had become a technical term in the Old Testament for the sending of a messenger with a special task. Although accepting responsibility and agreeing to accomplish what is asked, the person of the messenger (whether divine or human) fades behind the importance of being so "formally" commissioned. *Attention is to be focused on the initiator and his concerns* (emphasis mine).[7]

Jesus is saying two seemingly contradictory things about these twelve disciples: First, He has given them power and authority to act on His behalf. What they say and do is to be perceived as Jesus' very own speech and actions. On the flip side, their personal concerns now fade in importance to Jesus' work and will for them. He has conferred absolute authority and absolute submission on them at the same time. This concept needs to be in the forefront of our minds when we read Jesus' teaching today.

Read aloud Luke 6:17–49.
What did Jesus do before He began to teach?

How are Jesus' blessings and woes considered countercultural even today?

How and why might the apostles have mistaken their new apostleship with a bright and prosperous future?

The teachers of the Law were not only the elite in a religious sense, they were also some of the wealthiest members of Palestinian society. They were revered and beloved by the people, as most held a sense of awe over their strict adherence to the Law along with their knowledge of it. At this point in Israel's history, less than 10 percent of the population was able to read.[8] So, on many levels these scribes and teachers of the Law were indeed the "blessed ones." Jesus says that when the kingdom of God comes, *expect the unexpected*.

In the next section of Jesus' sermon to this large crowd, He implores them to *do the unexpected*. Jesus gives three reasons why:

- Your reward will be great
- You will be sons of the Most High
- He is kind to the ungrateful and evil, and He is merciful

Expect the unexpected. Do the unexpected. *Receive the unexpected*. Jesus invites the entire crowd into an even greater relationship with Himself than apostleship. You will be received as a child of the Most High. This isn't a relationship He offers only to the twelve apostles; this was an invitation to everyone in the crowd. Under Judaism, a son not only represented his father and held the authority to act on his behalf, a son had an intimacy with his father that an emissary or apostle did not. Over and over again, Jesus is going to bring things back to our heart. He does that here, first by telling a parable. The teachers of the Law insisted that their role was to consistently inform the masses how they were not measuring up to the demands of the Law. They viewed the people as disobedient and rebellious children, which was the reason God had not yet redeemed Israel from oppression.

Jesus is shedding light on their actions, suggesting that they are highlighting the tiniest of infractions against their traditions (specks), while ignoring their gross negligence of the spirit of the law in their judgmental and critical spirits toward the people (logs). Jesus insists they must become like Him: compassionate and willing to serve.

He now expounds on this teacher/student relationship by using the example of fruit. If these teachers of the Law were indeed good in their teaching, they would be producing good fruit in the lives of the people. The very fact that they insist their followers are sinful and bad negates the goodness within themselves. Jesus is being extremely controversial here, while at the same time using dry humor. He is going to conclude with a drastic warning: those teachers and their system of instruction are about to come to ruin.

So what does any of this have to do with us today? Jesus implores His audience to examine themselves. He is calling for them to cease concerning themselves with the sin and injustice others exhibit and instead focus on becoming like Him, with the promise of an intimate relationship with Him. Stop comparing yourself to everyone else and focus on becoming more engaged with Me. In other words, I want your heart—I want relationship with you. And when you become engaged with Me, you can expect the unexpected.

I have to admit, I waste a lot of energy worrying about people's behavior. When I do focus on what other people are doing—or not doing—it generally leads to evil assumptions and thoughts about them. It seldom compels me to do the unexpected for them. If anything, it causes me to pull away from them. How many people across the centuries have forsaken Jesus' command to fellowship within the church due to judgment of others' behavior?

How many times have you heard people rant, "The church is full of hypocrites!"?

Or on the flip side been told that someone left the church because someone wounded them there or failed to live up to their expectations? How does the church become an unexplainable place, infused with the love of Christ? When sincere followers do their best to seek Christ rather than continually look around them in comparison.

I love Jesus' teaching. He so very seldom tells us what to do—more often than not He simply points out how things are. Here is only one such beautiful example. If we live in a state of expectancy toward God, we'll have little time to concern ourselves with how others aren't measuring up to our expectations. When we expect God to do the unexpected for us, we will be so much more willing to do the unexpected for others. And Jesus promises us that if we are willing to follow His example in this, we will receive something even greater in the end. What a promise!

Part of that promise is that we will rest on a firm, solid foundation in this life. Not shaky, shifting emotions that crush us when someone fails to meet our expectations. No crumbling in a heap when someone has disappointed or betrayed us. He promises unexpected strength and stability in the midst of life's storms.

Let's pause and think about the truth of this teaching in Jesus' own life. God clothed in human flesh has left the glory of heaven and come down to dusty and dirty earth—expect the unexpected. He is going to suffer and die a horrible death—do the unexpected. He is going to conquer sin and death, returning to glory to rule and reign for eternity and offering to bring us with Him—receive the unexpected.

Have you ever thought about your expectations of Jesus? Do you believe He is trustworthy to provide for your needs physically, emotionally, and spiritually?

Are you like me and tend to spend too much time focusing on others' behavior rather than the goodness and trustworthiness of God?

How would expecting the unexpected from God change the way you are willing to do the unexpected for others?

Jesus promised His disciples that they would receive the unexpected—far more than what they could ever give—in return for their pursuit of Him. If you are struggling to believe that today, I invite you to pause and sit at His feet, asking Him to reveal Himself to you and build your trust in His promises. I know He has some work to do in my own heart in this area.

WEEK 3 | DAY 5
STUDY THE SIGNS
LUKE 7:1–35

I love the advice Andy Stanley gave at the 2018 West Coast Catalyst Conference: "Never underestimate the power of a great question!" Luke consistently highlights why Jesus could boldly make claims about Who He Was. Namely, it was because of the things He did. Luke doesn't stop there, though—he also forces us to examine our own hearts and answer Jesus' great question: Who do we believe Him to be?

Read aloud Luke 7:1–10.
What is the problem presented here?

For what reason do the Jews tell Jesus He should respond to this request?

Since the centurion was a Gentile and Jesus was a Jew, the Jewish law forbade entry into a Gentile home. So, how did the centurion propose Jesus solve this problem?

How did Jesus respond to the centurion's suggestion?

Okay, stick with me here. We're going to go right into the next story and then explore them together.

What is the problem presented to Jesus here?

What prompted Jesus to solve this problem?

What miracle did Jesus perform?

How did the people who witnessed it respond?

When I was a sophomore in college, my grandmother was diagnosed with cancer. A well-meaning friend approached me one day on campus imploring me to have faith that God would heal my grandmother. "Oh, He's going to heal her, all right!" I replied, "He's going to take her home to heaven!" My friend was distraught by this response and insisted I should have more faith. He then emphatically declared that if I lacked faith, God most certainly would not heal her.

I have met a lot of well-meaning Christians over the course of my life. They insist that if we keep the faith, God will answer our prayers in the way that we want. In fact, they will often cite this story as a proof text for their theological assumption. Jesus marveled at the centurion's faith and was therefore moved to action. If that is true, then how do they explain the story which immediately follows it?

After Jesus heals the centurion's servant, He and His disciples leave Capernaum and begin heading toward Nain—and there is a great crowd following Jesus, we are told. The distance between the two cities is about twenty-five miles, so it would have taken most of the day to arrive. As they approach the city, they are met by another crowd. Mourners surround a weeping widow who is followed by neighbors carrying a palette on which lies her deceased son.

Behind her, the entire village would follow, as was the custom, as they carried the body outside the town to a tomb, where they would wrap his body and leave him to rest. All the townspeople somberly process the hopelessness of the widow's situation.

Not only is this widow pierced with grief, she now has no one to care for her, unless she has another family member with the means to do so. Women in first-century Palestine did not usually hold jobs. Without a son to care for her, she would be relegated to begging for survival. It is this hopeless and helpless scene that moves Jesus to compassion and He stops the entourage. I wonder if He thought of His own mother in this scene.

There is no exchange between the widow and Jesus, merely a command to stop weeping. Jesus did not need to ask the details of the woman's situation—the solemnity and agony of the villagers, along with the regular funeral customs, informed those watching of the extremity of the situation. And Jesus raises her son from the dead.

No request for Him to do so by the mother. No begging for a miracle. No assertion that she believes Jesus can fix her situation. Just a compassionate King righting her injustice. Jesus never expected her to exercise faith in order for Him to raise her son from the dead.

God did take my grandmother home to heaven just a few weeks after my exchange about faith and healing with my friend. What my friend didn't know is that this was not my grandmother's first battle with cancer. She had initially been diagnosed over ten years before. Every Sunday after church, I would go with her to a kneeling bench just in front of the altar and our minister would anoint her head with oil, while an elder and I knelt down on each side of her holding her hands.

Every Sunday she would pray the same prayer. "Lord, please allow me to remain on this earth long enough to fulfill my wifely duty to Jack. When that time is finished, I am ready to go home." God answered that prayer and healed my grandmother's cancer. She had lived cancer-free for ten years and buried her husband as she had asked. Less than three weeks after burying him, she learned that her cancer had returned. I knew she wanted to go home. I had resolute faith that Jesus would welcome her home.

Unlike the Jews who insisted Jesus perform a miracle out of duty for the centurion's generosity, or my friend who insisted Jesus would keep my grandmother with me for a longer time if I only exhibited enough faith, this mourning widow received a miracle for no other reason than the mercy and compassion of God. Which leads us to Luke's last point in this grouping of stories: Who do you believe Jesus is?

Read aloud Luke 7:18–35.

What did the messengers of John the Baptist ask Jesus?

What was happening at the exact hour of their arrival?

How did Jesus answer their question?

John is trying to figure out who Jesus is. He thought He was the Messiah. In fact, he was sure of it, but his faith is beginning to waver. Now he sits in a prison cell and wonders why Jesus isn't ushering in His kingdom. If we look carefully at these last two miracles, we can see that Jesus has just ushered in the very kingdom He described in Luke 6 in His sermon! And while John is questioning who Jesus is, the crowds most likely are as well, so Jesus addresses the issue.

Jesus asks them some questions—some great questions:

What did you go out to the wilderness to see?

> A reed blowing around?
> A man in fine clothing?
> A prophet?

When Herod Antipas minted coins for his portion of the empire, he put reeds on them. It symbolized the fertility and prosperity of Israel. Jesus' question about a reed could have referred to an earthly, political king, possibly a dig at Herod for being overly influenced by Rome. Jesus also might have been saying that John the Baptist was *not* like a reed that would bend in the wind.

Next, Jesus refers to the rich in His mention of one dressed in fine clothing—or probably the wealthiest of the Palestinian community—which, as we already stated, would have included the scribes, Pharisees, and teachers of the Law. Jesus is indirectly asking them pointed questions:

> Are you looking for a king to overthrow Herod and set up a new earthly kingdom?
> Are you looking for a world system that honors wealth and power?
> Or are you looking for a prophet who will point you to God?

Then He follows up His questions with a strong messianic reference.

Read Malachi 3:1–2 and compare it with Luke 7:27.
How does Jesus describe John? What does Jesus say about those in His kingdom in Luke 7:28?

Describe the two responses to Jesus' statements outlined in Luke 7:29–30.

The marketplace was the common gathering place within a community. Children would often gather together and play while their parents shopped. Jesus claims that these teachers of the Law are like unhappy children who refuse to join in the childhood games. They are pouting in the corner. They are upset because John was too much of an ascetic. They are upset because Jesus is too much the life of the party (vv. 33–34). No matter what game is being played, they refuse to join in.

Write Luke 7:35 below.

Wisdom in Jewish culture was often personified as a woman. Jesus is inviting everyone present to look around at the crowd following Him. If He is teaching something false, why is He followed by so many? If the way of the teachers of the Law is correct, where are their followers? Jesus insists that those who are truly wise will recognize who He is. So let's ask ourselves some great questions:

Have you recognized Jesus? Do you believe He offers you kindness and mercy with you doing nothing to deserve it?

Have you recognized that continually comparing yourself to everyone else results in destructive disillusionment?

Have you recognized that unabashed faith in the kindness and mercy of God leaves Jesus marveling at you?

Never underestimate the power of a great question. These were some tough questions today, but their power lies in bringing us to the feet of Jesus asking Him to search our hearts. I want to become a person free from the comparison trap and who makes Jesus marvel—how about you?

unexplainable
TEACHING

THE MANY FACETS OF FAITH

LUKE 8:1–56

Jesus was a strong proponent of women, inviting them into activities reserved only for men.

Record the names of the three women mentioned by name who traveled with Jesus in His ministry according to Luke 8:1–3.

We are going to see something else extraordinary about Mary Magdalene as Luke's gospel unfolds, so I wanted to make specific mention of her here. These women traveling alongside of the disciples may not seem all that revolutionary to us in twenty-first-century America, where men and women coexist in workplaces and worship venues, but in Jesus' day women and men were consistently separated. By and large, women were considered property and allowed very few freedoms.

They had different areas within the temple where they worshiped. It would have been extremely countercultural for these women to intermix with His disciples. What blesses me even more is how Luke highlights these significant women by specifically mentioning them right before a series of stories presenting the unique privileges Jesus offered to His followers, implying their inclusion in them.

If we read through the entire chapter of Luke 8, it seems like it jumps all over the place. What is the consistent thread Luke is weaving in all of these stories about Jesus? Luke is emphasizing relationship. He is showing us specific things Jesus offers to those who are His followers. He also issues a warning to those who are merely seeking something *from* Him, rather than seeking *to know Him*.

Read aloud Luke 8:4–15.

Who did Jesus speak this parable to and how well was it understood?

To whom does Jesus fully explain the parable?

How does Jesus describe the heart of the "crop producers"?

This is key to understanding why Jesus says He speaks in parables. He is contrasting those who merely seek something from Him rather than those who are seeking to truly submit themselves to Him.

The word "good" He uses to describe the crop producers is the Hebrew word *tob*. "The theological idea is that *God is good*: for He is morally perfect, and gloriously generous." It further conveys, "Man is good, and things are good, just so far as they conform to the will of God."⁹

What is Jesus saying? Many are flocking to Him out of selfish motivation. They are not coming to Him with pure hearts but divided ones. They have a "What's in this for me?" attitude. They want something from Him, but they don't want to truly follow Him and conform to His teaching. The motivation of their heart will determine how the seeds Jesus is sowing will react in the soil of their heart. Jesus emphasizes His point in His next illustration.

Read aloud Luke 8:16–18 and record verse 18 below.

Let's make sure we effectively couple this with the story just told. Jesus is sowing seed. He is also bringing light to a dark world. Those who truly seek Him can expect Him to make use of the seed He has planted and the light He has placed within them. This isn't a proverbial guilt trip that we need to tell others about Jesus—which we do. But that isn't His point. We don't have to worry if Jesus is going to make use of the redemption, salvation, and giftedness He has brought to our lives. We can count on Him doing so if we are submitted to His leading.

But those with dishonest and selfish hearts will see their true intentions revealed. Because they only seek to benefit from Jesus' works, the truths of His words will remain hidden to them. And while they follow Him to witness a miracle or hear interesting sermons, they'll ditch Him as soon as it costs them something.

In verse 18 Jesus is not talking about salvation being taken away; He is referring to His eventual departure. These people will no longer have Him physically in their presence. But to those who truly seek Him, indeed more would be given. Currently, Jesus is with them bodily, but after His death and resurrection, He will send the Holy Spirit who actually dwells inside of His followers, equipping and empowering them to follow Jesus despite His departure. Jesus never wastes anything. That which He gives us, we can trust He will make good and perfect use of: our knowledge of Him, our experience with Him, and our service to Him.

Read aloud Luke 8:19–21.
Who was looking for Jesus? How does Jesus add to His definition of who makes up His family?

What is the common thread you see in Luke 8:15 and Luke 8:21?

Jesus' true followers are those who hear His Word, retain it, and put it into practice, producing a crop. You don't become a true follower of Jesus by birth, denomination, the town you grew up in, or who you happen to know. Jesus reveals His truth to His true followers and they seek Him, not just what they can get from Him.

How do you become a true follower of Jesus?
God's plan of salvation is as easy as ABC!

Admit you are a sinner in need of a Savior. Romans 3:23 tells us, "For all have sinned and fall short of God's glory."

Believe Jesus came to die on the cross for your sins and rose again to save you from sin and death. "For I delivered to you as of first importance what I also received," Paul says in 1 Corinthians 15:3–4. "That Christ died for our sins . . . that he was buried, that he was raised on the third day."

Commit to follow Him with your life, with the promise that He is with you always, guiding and directing your steps. Jesus said, "All authority in heaven and on earth has been given to me. Go therefore and make disciples of all nations, baptizing them in the name of the Father and of the Son and of the Holy Spirit, teaching them to observe all that I have commanded you. And behold, I am with you always, to the end of the age" (Matt. 28:18–20).

Yes, it really is that simple! Please tell someone you know who is a follower of Christ about your decision. They can help you continue to grow in your relationship with Jesus. And please, email me at erica@ericawiggenhorn.com. I'd love to be one of the first to welcome you into the family of God!

Read aloud Luke 8:22–39.

Over what two things was Jesus' power demonstrated, and who specifically witnessed this?

How did the townspeople respond when they heard the story about Jesus' power?

Who was left behind to continually remind them of God's power?

Here again we see special disclosure to the disciples who were with Him in the boat. They alone had been given secrets to the kingdom: the truth of His words and witnesses of His power. In the next story, we are going to see Jesus hand select three of His followers to witness an even greater disclosure of His unexplainable power.

Jesus has come back across the lake to Capernaum. This city has served as His base of operations up to this point in His ministry. It is also the home of Peter, Andrew, James, and John: four of His disciples. He has performed many miracles here and developed a large following as a teacher. Another teacher in town, the synagogue ruler, pleads with Jesus to perform a miracle.

What's interesting about this and easy to miss, is that Jairus waits until his daughter is to the point of death before he beseeches Jesus for help. There were most certainly many days Jesus had been in Capernaum healing the sick and Jairus could have come much sooner than now. Or he could have easily sent messengers to nearby Galilean towns in search of Jesus. Continually surrounded by giant crowds now, it would not have been difficult to track Him down. Why had he waited until he was at the end of his rope to ask for help?

Well, when you look at Luke's emphasis in all these accounts, it is easy to understand why. It may be that Jairus had not been a seeker of Jesus, but at a desperate time, he was the seeker of a miracle.

Read aloud Luke 8:40–56.

What miracle did Jairus seek from Jesus?

What happened while Jesus was on the way to Jairus's house?

What question did Jesus ask?

How did Peter answer Him?

What did Jesus insist?

How did the woman respond?

This woman also wanted a miracle from Jesus. And in her desperation, she received one. But Jesus doesn't only want us to witness His power, He also wants us to experience His love. He insisted that He have the opportunity to meet the one so desperate for His touch.

Let's really think about this. Was Jesus really unaware of who touched Him? Of course not! He is God. He knew exactly who it was, which is why Luke emphasizes that the woman knew she could not go unnoticed.

I have heard it said that Jesus' miracles were performed to support His claims. I believe that wholeheartedly, but I think there is a deeper and more personal reason for them as well—something unexplainable. Jesus' miracles were not merely an authentication of His identity, but an invitation to intimacy. His miracles opened the door to truly understand the wonders of His person and the vastness of His power. And as Jesus locked eyes with the woman, I believe His gaze asked a simple question to her soul, "Did you just want the healing or do you also want the Healer?" Jesus could have allowed her to go home, healed and whole, without ever encountering intimacy with Jesus' person, only an experience of His power, but instead, Jesus didn't merely offer her His power, He offered her Himself. She had the opportunity to hear His voice and was affirmed for her faith.

In the middle of this exchange between Jesus and the woman, what message was told to Jairus?

Who specifically went with Jesus into Jairus's house?

How did the mourners respond to Jesus?

How did the child's parents respond to this miracle?

What did Jesus command Jairus and his wife not to do?

The Greek word that Luke uses here for "amazed" in Luke 8:56 is significant. Listen to this definition: "it usually expresses terror before Yahweh or at His judgments: Jer. 4:9; Ez. 26:16."[10] Luke intimates in the use of this word that Jairus recognized Jesus' power originating from Yahweh. And interestingly, Jesus commanded him not to tell anyone. He was the synagogue ruler, the teacher of the town. He was told *not* to tell his town, but the healed demonized man was. Why the difference?

Let's go back to Luke's point in this chapter. Those who truly seek Jesus will have His Word and power revealed to them. Those who don't, won't. The people of Capernaum had witnessed Jesus' power and heard His teaching countless times. Yet they laughed at Him when He suggested Jairus' daughter could be healed. The Gerasenes on the other side of the lake knew nothing of Jesus other than this one unexplainable event: a demon-possessed man restored and healed. They had not rejected Jesus. In their fear they had sent Him away, but with more time and understanding, maybe they would eventually come to believe in Him.

Now it's time to examine our own relationship with Jesus.
Do we merely want something from Jesus, or do we want intimacy with Jesus?

Do we have undisclosed agendas and expectations of Him?

Do we trust Jesus to make our lives fruitful and make use of the light He has placed within us, or have we given Him a demand or a stipulation on how and where He must or must not place us in service to Him?

Are we content with a healing, or are we in pursuit of the Healer?

To His true followers, Jesus reveals His truth, demonstrates His power, and reveals His true mission, inviting us to become part of it. To these He gives the secrets to the kingdom. Pause and imagine Jesus approaching you right now at exactly the place you are sitting, holding this book before you. Listen to His whisper, "Come here, child, come closer to Me. Let Me tell you a secret . . . "

THE SECRETS OF SERVICE IN THE KINGDOM

LUKE 9

I think one of the things that I appreciate most about Luke's writing style is that he continually reemphasizes his points. For this girl, who is often not the sharpest nail in the shed, another blow of the hammer helps a lot! Do you remember the points Luke made yesterday in Luke 8? Those who were truly ready to follow Christ—to seek relationship with Him—would be given the secrets of the kingdom, witness the power of the kingdom, and be invited to join Jesus in His work and mission of building the kingdom.

Luke illustrated these truths for us in both parables and miracles. Today, Luke is going to show us in living color what the fulfillment of these promises of Jesus looks like! Grip your hammer firmly, because we have got some amazing truth to pound through today!

Read aloud Luke 9:1–10.

What specifically did Jesus give His apostles?

What did He specifically command them to do?

Based on verses 7–9, how widespread do you think their ministry was?

Where did they go once they returned?

The disciples have just served in Jesus' power. Now they must learn to serve in His humility.

Read aloud Luke 9:10–17.
What problem needed solving?

What was the apostles' solution?

What did Jesus suggest?

This is the only miracle of Jesus recorded by all four gospel writers. What is so significant about this particular event that they all felt compelled to include it in their individual sketches of Jesus? Well, not to be critical of the disciples, but this miracle in particular, probably more so than most others, had to do with them.

Jesus had invited them into His work and His mission. They were being sent to serve and care for people, and that was going to require tremendous faith to live out. Could it be the twelve basketfuls left over implied that after feeding everyone else first, the disciples now had the opportunity to sit down and eat themselves?

At this point in Jesus' ministry He has literally given them pieces of Himself: namely, His power and authority. The following year after He would be crucified and resurrected, He would give them all of Himself through the indwelling of the

Holy Spirit—including the continued work of the kingdom. This beautiful word picture is Jesus' invitation to trust and receive Him fully: His power, His authority, and His mission. The disciples don't understand that yet, as we will see in a few verses, but later I believe they realized what Jesus was teaching them here—and why this miracle became so important to them both individually and collectively.

Read aloud Luke 9:18–27.

According to Jesus' conversation with His disciples, how certain were the crowds of Jesus' true identity?

How certain were the apostles?

According to this conversation, what kind of Messiah would Jesus be?

What would following Him require?

What did Jesus promise them at the end of this conversation?

Jesus affirms that He indeed is the Messiah they believe Him to be. What they don't yet understand is that He is a suffering Messiah. He will establish His kingdom with a sacrifice. And eight days later three of His disciples witness firsthand the glory and power of the kingdom.

Read aloud Luke 9:28–37.

Who did Jesus take with Him up onto the mountain to pray?

Who appeared with Jesus, and what did they discuss?

What does Peter suggest they do, and what comment does Luke insert regarding this idea?

What words did the three hear? Who was speaking?

This is Luke's magnum opus establishing Jesus' identity. In fact, Luke references an incredibly significant event to accentuate Jesus' mission.

In Luke 9:31, when Moses and Elijah discuss Jesus' "departure," Luke uses the word "exodus." The exodus was the single most important event in Israel's history. God called Moses to deliver His people from Egypt—the exodus—and take them to their promised land, which is now Israel. He established them as a nation through Moses, made a covenant with them through the giving of the law up on Mount Sinai, while He descended on Moses in a cloud (notice any similarities in this story?) and promised that a prophet even greater than Moses would be sent to restore their nation when they wandered away from God. Now here's where the similarity in these stories becomes exceedingly striking:

Write out Deuteronomy 18:15.

Circle the word that the people were to do in regard to this prophet. Recall Jesus' admonition to His disciples in Luke 8:18.

Peter gets that he is witnessing the kingdom of God on this mountain. In fact, during the Feast of Ingathering, the Jewish people would build booths, not only to commemorate past events in Israel's history, but also in anticipation of the coming of the kingdom.

> For more on the Feast of Ingathering along with the ties between Moses's ministry and Jesus', visit *Come to the Table* at www.ericawiggenhorn.com.

What he seems to have forgotten is Jesus' earlier admonition that He is going to have to suffer before the kingdom becomes fully established. And what Peter even more conveniently forgot was that he was going to have to suffer also. He isn't being a very good listener. So Jesus is going to have to repeat a few points to these guys in hopes that they start to get it. This is where Luke goes next in his narrative.

Read aloud Luke 9:37–45.

What were the disciples unable to do?

What did Jesus command them to do at the beginning of verse 44?

What did Jesus again warn them about?

How well did they understand what Jesus was saying?

Just like the feeding of the five thousand, the disciples had to be 100 percent dependent on the faithfulness and power of God to carry out Jesus' mission. Did they really lack faith in Jesus' ability to cast out demons? I doubt it. They had already witnessed Him going head to head with the forces of darkness countless times and defeating them with a word. What they doubted was whether or not Jesus could overcome the forces of darkness through them. Did they truly hold Jesus' power and authority as His messengers?

Interesting things happen when people have been given power or authority. We see this now unfold in the attitudes of the disciples.

Read aloud Luke 9:46–56.

What were the disciples arguing about?

What concerned John?

What did the disciples offer to do in response to Jesus' rejection?

Once people have been given a position, they want to know how it relates to everyone else. They also want to know that their position is secure. John wonders if their position as the chosen Twelve may be usurped by someone else.

Lastly, people often feel tempted to exercise the power their position brings them: hence, the judgment over those who are rejecting Jesus. They still aren't listening. Having Jesus' power and authority means He is inviting them to suffer and serve now in exchange for future glory later. Again, Jesus tries to get their attention and divulge the true secrets of the kingdom. Listen up, guys!

Read aloud Luke 9:57–62 and note each man's offer and how Jesus responds:

MAN #1	JESUS' RESPONSE
_____	_____
_____	_____
_____	_____

MAN #2	JESUS' RESPONSE
_____	_____
_____	_____
_____	_____

MAN #3	JESUS' RESPONSE
_____	_____
_____	_____
_____	_____

Jesus once referred to Herod Antipas as a fox (Luke 13:32). Jesus' kingdom does not bring power and palaces to His disciples; it could bring poverty. The rewards come later. Burying one's father represented the supreme duty of a Jewish son. Jesus' kingdom surpasses the highest of familial expectations.

To go back and say goodbye to one's family represented a return to seek their family's blessing to leave their farm or trade and go follow Jesus as a disciple. The point is that nearly every Jewish father is going to tell his son, "No!" to such a request.

The son's duty is at home, tending the farm or the trade of his earthly father, to care for him in his old age and to one day bury him. While the request sounds noble, in actuality it is a convenient excuse not to follow Jesus. I have too much earthly responsibility to concern myself with a heavenly kingdom.

The farmer with his plow always must look ahead or he cannot plow straight. If you decide to be part of Jesus' kingdom, there's no turning back. You're either all in and willing to forsake all else, or you are unwilling to follow Him at all. Can you see any correlation between these men's responses and the parable of the sower back in Luke 8?

This chapter represents a turning point in Luke's gospel. He has systematically proven that Jesus is indeed the Messiah. He is both divine and human. He is calling His disciples into an intimate relationship with Him in which He shares the secrets of the kingdom, invites them to work alongside of Him in the establishment of His kingdom, and confers on them power and authority over the forces of evil and darkness that will come against His kingdom. The most unexplainable part is that Jesus invites you and me to this same relationship, work, and power today. If we will only pay attention and listen . . .

WEEK 4 | DAY 3
THE PURPOSE OF THE POWER
LUKE 10:1–24

Over the last two days, when we've talked about the secrets of the kingdom, the power of the kingdom, and an invitation to join in the work of the kingdom, Jesus spoke primarily to the Twelve. So does that mean that these promises and authority were only given to them as His special apostles? I don't think so, because today we are going to see Jesus also extended that invitation to seventy-two more of His disciples. But before He sends them out, He gives a few specific commands.

Read aloud Luke 10:1–12 and note the first thing Jesus told them to do:

The only preparation required of them was spiritual readiness—they took no provisions with them. Jesus is telling them to be prepared to be on the move constantly.

Once they arrived, they remained and received hospitality. This can be difficult sometimes. We want to go serve, but then we don't want to receive in return. We feel uncomfortable when those we are serving desire to show us gratitude. Or we are afraid to hang around and find out how they really felt about our service. Do you notice how many of these commands require relationship among the disciples and those they are serving? I think we've cemented the fact that relationship is more important to Jesus than service.

In light of the thousands of people crowding around Jesus daily, I find it so incredible that Jesus says that the workers are few. Of all those people following Him from town to town, why weren't there enough of them willing to go back to their villages and prepare the way for Him to come visit there? When we ponder this, we can understand Jesus' teaching in Luke 8 and what He meant by His "true followers." They were eager to witness His power, but shrank back from obeying Him and joining Him in His kingdom mission.

Read aloud Luke 10:13–16.

Based on Jesus' description of these cities, how do you think Jesus expected these seventy-two to be received?

Chorazin, Bethsaida, and Capernaum were Galilean cities and part of Israel. Sodom represents the most wicked city in Israel's history (see Genesis 18–19). Tyre and Sidon were sister cities ruled by the Phoenicians. We mentioned previously that Jezebel was the Sidonian princess who was married to Israel's wicked King Ahab.

As a follower of Jesus, I too have been sent to go out into the world ahead of Jesus. He is returning, and I am His messenger. And if you are a follower of Jesus, then so are you! Jesus commands us to pray for more workers to go ahead of Him. And He doesn't send His workers alone, but in pairs.

Do you have partners in ministry? Do you regularly ask God for them? Are you willing to be a partner to someone else? Scripture makes it clear: there is great power in partnership. Again, partnership goes back to relationship. This is what Jesus emphasizes next.

Read aloud Luke 10:17–24.

Why are the seventy-two filled with joy?

Phil Yancey in *Rumors of Another World* describes the scene like this:

> To his followers, Jesus hinted at the effect they were having on the world beyond their vision. "I saw Satan fall like lightning from heaven," he told one group as they returned from a mission trip. They had been walking over hot sand, knocking on doors, asking to see the sick, announcing the coming of Jesus. All their actions took place in the visible world, which they could touch,

smell, and see. Jesus, with supernatural insight, saw that those actions in the visible world were having a startling impact on the invisible world. The world we live in is not an either/or world. What I do as a Christian . . . is not exclusively supernatural or natural, but both working at the same time. Perhaps if Jesus stood in the flesh beside me, murmuring phrases like "I saw Satan fall" whenever I acted in his name, I would remember better the connections between the two worlds.[11]

What does Jesus tell them to rejoice over?

What has God the Father handed over to Jesus?

Jesus is emphasizing that the tangible, earthly evidence of His kingdom before their eyes is only a shadow of the glory of Jesus' kingdom in the spiritual realm. Jesus tells them: Do not rejoice in what you are able to do . . . rejoice in the identity of who you are. And never forget that when you act in my name and power, you are bringing a touch of heaven to earth.

Jesus knew the Father fully knew Him. He took great comfort that He was fully known and fully loved. Forever loved. Not loved until He messed up or something or someone else came along, but eternally loved.

You, precious one, are fully known and fully loved. Forever loved. Faithfully loved, regardless of what you do or don't do. Let that sink in. Don't just keep reading on to the next point without basking in this truth for a moment.

> Jesus says you are fully known.
> I see you.
> I know the dreams in your soul.

I know the thoughts in your head.

I know your gifts and your skills.

I know the feelings in your heart: loneliness, longing and loss, bitterness, envy, and anger.

I know the harsh words spoken.

I know the secret pleasures in which you indulge.

I know them all, and I love you.

Describe a relationship in which a person is loved but not known:

Describe a relationship in which a person is known but not loved:

You are fully known and fully loved. How does this truth soothe your soul most deeply?

Think of all of the attitudes and emotions of the twelve apostles we have explored the past three days:

Where does *my* relationship with Jesus stack up compared to everyone else's? *Am I the most important?*

Sure, I have a special relationship with Jesus now, but will I always, or will Jesus invite someone else to take my place?

I know Jesus can do powerful things, but can He really do those same powerful things *through me?*

What if I can't perform? What if I don't measure up? *Will He love me even then?*

I don't know what goes on in your head on a daily basis, but I can easily say that I have rolled these exact same questions around my heart and mind on more occasions than I'd like to admit. So let's look at how Jesus answered those hidden questions of the heart.

Fully known and fully loved—forever. This is the relationship Jesus offers. Unexplainable.

Before we close our books today, let's pause and express our thanks to Jesus for His unexplainable love. Let's confess the places in which we are having trouble believing and receiving that love, asking Him to sow seeds of faith and shine light on any lies we are accepting as truth.

WEEK 4 | DAY 4
RATIONALIZATION AND RESPONSIBILITY
LUKE 10:25–42

If I'm blatantly honest about my struggle to follow Jesus, I can sum it up in two words: rationalization and responsibility. What do I mean by that? I rationalize half-hearted obedience and I prioritize perceived responsibilities over relationships, especially my relationship with Jesus. Today, we are going to meet two people who were experts at this and how Jesus responds to them. And maybe, we'll see a little of ourselves in the encounters.

Read aloud Luke 10:25–29.

Who questioned Jesus, and what did he ask Him?

What was his motive?

How did Jesus respond?

In what way does Jesus respond with authority over the one asking the question?

What led the man to press Jesus for further explanation?

This man wanted to limit those he needed to "love as himself." He wanted to rationalize to whom he needed to be a neighbor. Jesus begins to tell him a story. Now, we can presume this was not a one-on-one conversation because Luke tells us he "stood up" to ask Jesus the question. This hints that he was sitting among a crowd and arose before asking the question to direct Jesus' attention toward him.

Read aloud Luke 10:30–37.
What happened to the man in the narrative?

Who passed by the man first? Second? Last?

List all the care the Samaritan provided for the man and the order in which he provided it:

-
-
-

What question did Jesus pose to the lawyer?

What command did He issue to him?

Since we don't regularly travel from Jerusalem to Jericho, nor do we understand exactly the complete word picture Jesus is painting before His audience, we need to step into first-century Palestine for a moment and truly take this apart. This road was notoriously dangerous, and robbers and bandits were a constant threat. Because the man was coming from Jerusalem, the Holy City where one went to worship God, and because Jesus is in Israel, talking to Jewish people, the audience would most likely assume the man is a fellow Jew. Jesus doesn't specifically tell us as He leaves the man's identity in obscurity, letting His audience place their assumptions into the storyline.

We know that there were pagan settlements and foreigners in Israel at this time, and a person's identity could be discerned either by speech or by clothing. Because this man is both stripped and unconscious, it is impossible to determine anything about him, other than the fact that he is a fellow human in need.

The priest passed by, presumably riding, since priests constituted part of the upper class of Israel and only the poor would walk seventeen miles. He is unable to ascertain the condition of the man. He cannot call out to him if the man is unconscious, and if he is already dead, the priest would defile himself going near enough to him to determine so. Then he would have to rend his garments and spend great expense in sacrifices for purification.

The priestly commandment to remain undefiled was unconditional, but the command to love your neighbor was conditional on the righteousness of the recipient. The listeners to the story would have expected the priest to continue riding by and even found him justified in doing so. A priest was not called to risk defilement. Jesus is not condemning the priest for his actions; rather, He is building up a case to open the hearers' ears and hearts to understand that the exhaustive nature of the letter of the law, to which had been added millennia of oral tradition, had, in actuality, resulted in a destruction in the spirit of the law—to exhibit the mercy and love of God.

Now, a Levite comes along next. Some scholars assert that due to the nature of this road, one is able to see who is traveling ahead of them for quite a distance, with an unobstructed view. Jerusalem is high upon a hill while Jericho is down within a valley, so you are traveling downhill the entire route. When listening to this story, we need to assume that the Levite was fully aware of the priest who had gone before him and passed by the man without offering aid.[12] The purification requirements for Levites were much less stringent than those for a priest, so the Levite could potentially stop without incurring as great a cost to himself to complete the proper cleansing. However, this would mean choosing a different response than his spiritual superior, the priest, had done, which would have proved very countercultural under the current religious system.

The third passerby comes as a shock. The drama unfolding seems to paint the picture of the group of men who would commonly officiate in the temple in Jerusalem: a priest, a Levite, and next a Jewish layman. Instead, Jesus takes a dramatic twist in the storyline: a Samaritan comes along. It is hard for us to wrap our minds around the racial hatred between the Jews of Israel and the Samaritans, but it was a long and sordid history, which led to much fighting and cruelty. The audience would have been shocked that Jesus chose someone so despised to be the hero of the tale. In doing so, He would have immediately evoked the wrath of His audience.

The Samaritan brings great risk on himself in returning to pay the man's debt, as the man's own family could seek out retribution against the Samaritan for coming into contact with their kindred Jew.

The conclusion the lawyer and the rest of the audience listening is pressed to make:

> I must *become* a neighbor to anyone in need. To fulfill the law means that I must reach out in costly compassion to all people, even to my enemies. The standard remains even though I can never fully achieve it. I cannot justify myself and earn eternal life.[13]

No amount of rationalization will lead to justification. I need Jesus to save me from my sinfulness. I cannot go and do likewise in my own power. This doesn't lead to rationalization of half-hearted obedience, but it should lead to a cry to Jesus to save me from myself.

Luke first shocks his readers by turning racial conceptions upside down. Next, he moves into gender roles.

Read aloud Luke 10:38–42.
What did Martha do for Jesus and His disciples?

What did Mary not do?

How did Martha feel about this?

Poor Martha. For centuries this hospitable woman has continually gotten a bad rap. Martha feels responsible to be a good host. But let's face it, this is a lot of work, especially without the luxury of modern conveniences. Martha doesn't own a microwave.

Then she takes a look at her sister. Mary's lounging at the feet of Jesus while Martha is slaving away in the kitchen. My real question is why none of the disciples offered to come in and take what little Martha had prepared and multiply it for her, or remind her that Jesus had miraculously fed five thousand men, not including all the women and children who had also happened to be there. He could easily handle the meal. She needed to release her perceived responsibilities and enjoy Jesus' presence.

Oh, how greatly I can relate to Martha! I get so distracted by duties and to-do lists. Martha heaped responsibilities on herself unnecessarily and missed out on the opportunity to just be with Jesus. But do you know what else Martha did? She heaped responsibilities and expectations on Mary also. In fact, I'm not even 100 percent convinced that Martha was upset about Mary not being in the kitchen. Maybe what upset her most was Mary's crazy idea that it was okay for her to sit at Jesus' feet among all the men as though she herself were one of this famed rabbi's students.

"She has no business being in there. A woman's place is in the kitchen, not out with the men!" fumed Martha: unrealistic expectations of herself and expectations on her sister Mary as to how she should act. Mary was boldly crossing gender roles and Martha wanted to know why Jesus was allowing it.

N. T. Wright explains, "To sit at someone's feet meant, quite simply, to be their student. And to sit at the feet of a rabbi was what you did if you wanted to be a rabbi yourself. There is no thought here of learning for learning's sake. Mary has quietly taken her place as a would-be teacher . . . . Mary stands for all those women who, when they hear Jesus speaking about the kingdom, know that God is calling them to listen carefully so that they can speak of it too."[14]

Why doesn't Jesus correct her for her brazenness?

Rationalization and responsibility. Both limit my relationship with Jesus. Both stifle the freedom to follow Him fully. Both place a heavier emphasis on doing than being. While I foolishly pursue them thinking they will provide helpful boundaries in decision-making, in actuality they subjugate me to the tyranny of self-imposed expectations. And in the case of Mary, we can choose to be limited by the expectations of others, or we can bring those limitations spoken over us to the feet of Jesus. Our Savior lived in complete trust and submission to His Father. He invites His followers to live that way too.

Which do you struggle with more: rationalization or responsibility? How so?

If you haven't figured it out yet, Jesus is most interested in a relationship with you: not your performance, your righteousness, or your knowledge. He wants your heart. He wants you to choose sitting at His feet over all else. He doesn't expect you to be perfect. And as we'll discover tomorrow, He invites us into beautiful relationship through prayer.

In fact, how about we start today? Let's pause for a few moments and sit at Jesus' feet. Share with Him the things on your heart. Ask Him to show you where you are rationalizing in your life and where you have placed unnecessary responsibilities upon yourself. Choose, today, the only thing that is necessary—relationship with Jesus. He can take care of your to-do list, even if it means feeding five thousand people.

WEEK 4 | DAY 5
THE POWER OF PRAYER
LUKE 11:1–27

Jesus' emphasis on relationship with Him, thus with God, and with our fellow human beings, has crossed several social boundaries the last couple of days. Jesus is going to cross even more boundaries today in His description of our relationship with His Father through prayer.

Jesus viewed prayer as a means to relationship. Prayer is not a way to gain favor with God, because Jesus insists we already have that. It is not to manipulate people or circumstances as though God were some sort of all-powerful genie who must grant our wish because we have said the correct words or done the right thing. (Incantation securing one's desired response from the gods was a common belief among pagans of Jesus' day in both the ancient Canaanite religions as well as both Greek and Roman mythology.)

Jesus presents prayer as a means to strengthen our relationship with God. We have confidence in prayer because of who our Father is, not because of how, what, when, or why we pray. Prayer is rooted in the power and character of God.

What is important to note also is that prior to this point, the disciples have witnessed Jesus praying at every significant event in His ministry. He prayed at His baptism (3:21), and before He chose the twelve apostles (6:12). They often saw Him withdraw alone to pray (5:16, 9:18), and He also prayed with others around to hear Him (9:28–29). Later in the gospel we will see Him make specific requests for Peter (22:32), before He goes to the cross (22:40–44) and even while hanging upon it (23:46).

This is not to imply that these were the only times Jesus prayed, for He certainly would have prayed during times of regular custom as a first century Jew—as He did in the synagogue at Nazareth (4:16–22). But Jesus' practice of pulling away to pray and crying out to God in significant moments awakened the disciples' realization that Jesus held a special relationship with God that invited Him into a place of communion with Him in prayer. He didn't just pray ritualistic prayers taught by the rabbis, He prayed personal prayers in direct response to the circumstances at hand.

The disciples already knew the rabbinic prayers—those conducted daily, each Sabbath, and during religious feasts. Every Jew knew them. So when the disciples asked Him to teach them how to pray, I believe what they were really asking Him was: teach us how to have intimacy with God the way You do in Your prayers, Jesus.

Read aloud Luke 11:1–4.

Write out the prayer Jesus modeled for His disciples below:

Circle the actions that He is petitioning God to do.

Underline the actions He is expecting the disciples to do.

What do you notice?

Prayer is about relationship with God, which then affects our relationships with one another. Next, Jesus tells a parable to help them understand this Father with whom they are seeking to connect.

Read aloud Luke 11:5–13.

What time of day does this incident occur, and what is the friend requesting?

In Palestinian culture, hospitality is greatly valued. To not offer a guest something to eat was unthinkable and tantamount to the greatest shame a host could heap upon themselves and their community.[15] Furthermore, if a host had an unexpected guest and his neighbor refused to aid him with food in order to provide hospitality, this would be exceedingly shameful, even at midnight when it would be pretty inconvenient to oblige. While many people like to insist this parable is about the neighbor's shamelessness, I think it is actually more about the Father's blamelessness.

The emphasis is not on the neighbor being obstinate and needing several appeals to open the door; Jesus is emphasizing that without question the neighbor will answer. The assumption is that he would never consider turning away from this legitimate need. And in order to prove his character, he will even give beyond what is requested. This is Jesus' next point.

What did the man initially ask his neighbor for?

Jesus says the neighbor is going to give him "whatever he needs," which is probably more than just bread, because a first-century hospitable host is going to serve their guest an entire meal, even if they arrive at midnight. Fish and eggs would be common elements in a meal in Jesus' day. While we frequently applaud the neighbor's persistence in asking, we must equally focus on Jesus' emphasis on the Father who answers our prayers. In Palestinian culture, the host is behaving according to societal expectations, as is the neighbor. So what is the best application? You have a good and kind Father; therefore, expect Him to act out of His good and kind character.

A type of fish resembling an eel or snake was often caught in the fishermen's nets, but was not edible. The white scorpion of the Palestinian desert coiled up could resemble an egg. But our heavenly Father's generosity goes beyond the responsiveness and offering of a blameless and noble neighbor. He provides for our spiritual and our physical needs.

What will the heavenly Father give us?

Why does Jesus mention the Holy Spirit here? Because the intimacy Jesus experiences with the Father is the same intimacy we will experience with the Holy Spirit living inside of us! This intimacy not only creates closeness in relationship, it provides an unexplainable source of power.

Read aloud Luke 11:14–28.
What conclusion did some people reach regarding Jesus' ability to cast out demons?

What illustration does Jesus give to demonstrate how illogical this would be?

The expression "finger of God" meant something significant to Jesus' audience. It referred to Moses's ability to initiate plagues against Egypt by God's power. These plagues were to be signs to Pharaoh of God's power and an invitation to obey Him and release His people Israel. However, the Egyptian magicians were able to copy some of the initial plagues performed by Moses using their secret arts.

But by the third plague, the magicians finally consented that Moses possessed a power they could no longer imitate, claiming that Moses performed his signs by "the finger of God" (see Ex. 8:19). Jesus' explanation that His own power to cast out demons is by the finger of God is no casual comparison. This is a huge claim totaling divine dispensation of power.

Jesus emphasizes that those who do not recognize Him as God's unique agent to usher in the kingdom are against Him or contrary to His work of bringing about the kingdom. There is no ambivalence when it comes to Jesus. Either you recognize Him as God or you are against Him. Many have said, "Well, I think he was a prophet. He was a moral teacher. He was the ultimate humanitarian." Those descriptors all sound well and good, but Jesus says, "If you don't accept Me as God, you are against Me."

This next paragraph sounds a bit foreboding. If this were true, then wouldn't it have been better for Jesus to just leave the one demon in the man to begin with? What in the world does He mean here? Verse 23 is a turning point in Jesus' explanation. Jesus has turned the emphasis away from the man to the entire crowd by using the term "whoever."

Jesus is currently "in the house," and He is cleaning things up and putting things in order by healing the sick, bringing sight to the blind, casting out demons, and preaching and teaching the Word of God. Meanwhile, the forces of darkness are being pushed back due to His presence. But when Jesus departs, they are going to return—Jesus does not mean individually to this man—but to the nation of Israel. Now that they have rejected His power, they will be worse off than they were before His arrival. Once they have forsaken relationship, Jesus warns, they will be left to fight alone against the forces of evil.

And in the following paragraph, Luke concludes his section of his gospel on relationships.

What did the woman yell out among the crowd?

How did Jesus respond?

Familial relationships were huge in Jesus' day. By and large, whatever family you were born into determined who and what you would become. If you weren't a Levite, there was no way you were going to become a priest. If your father was a Pharisee, you had a good chance of becoming a scribe, rabbi, or Pharisee also. Carpenters usually reared carpenters. Fishermen beget fishermen, and so on.

The people of Israel also relied heavily on their birthright as children of Abraham. This afforded them a special relationship with God as His chosen people. Jesus sums up those who have the most treasured relationship on earth: those who hear the Word of God and obey it.

How regularly is your relationship with God deepened through the practice of prayer?

When you approach your heavenly Father in prayer, are you mindful of His blamelessness, goodness, and generosity or afraid that you might be "bothering Him at midnight"?

Do you live in the confidence that your intimacy with God, through the indwelling of the Holy Spirit, provides a source of power in your life, allowing it to look unexplainable to the outside world?

If blessedness comes from hearing the Word of God and obeying it, as Jesus insists, exactly how blessed would you consider your life at the moment?

Jesus has called us into an unexplainable relationship with the Father, Himself and the Holy Spirit. Within this intimate relationship, Jesus reveals the secrets of His kingdom to us. This relationship produces power in our lives. This power enables us to join Him in the work of the kingdom, bringing the hope and healing of Christ's love to a dark and desperate world. This relationship compels us to invite others into Jesus' kingdom as well, and until they are ready to accept the invitation, we pray, "Father, hallowed be Your name. Your kingdom come."

AN
unexplainable
KINGDOM

WHOM SHALL I FEAR?

LUKE 12:1–48

When I first became a Christian and learned about the idea of the Trinity—Father, Son, and Holy Spirit—I kind of had a mixed-up view of God. I thought of Father God as being mean and harsh and Jesus being kind and gentle. I really didn't have a well-formed idea regarding the Holy Spirit because we didn't talk about Him much in our particular denomination, other than when we recited the Apostles' Creed, and then we called Him a ghost!

When the disciples wanted to know how to connect with the Father with the same kind of intimacy that Jesus modeled in prayer, Jesus emphasized the kindness and goodness of the Father. Intimacy with God was a foreign concept to the Jews. Even though because of God's covenant with them as His chosen people they believed they had greater intimacy with God than any other people group, they still viewed God's favor as tenuous based on their adherence to the Law. They also viewed God's favor as being reserved for the learned and the most pious, not the common Jew. Jesus is teaching the disciples about an intimacy with the Father that would have been new to them.

As Christians today, we take great comfort in our intimacy with God. We are taught that we can bring any concern, no matter how small, before a loving Father who holds deep care for us. And because of the blood of Jesus covering our sin and reconciling us to our Father, this is 100 percent true. However, just as the ancient Jews often held misconceptions about God's distance and harshness, sometimes as modern-day Christians, we can diminish our awe of God's holiness and forget the vast gulf that once existed between our Creator and His creation due to our sinfulness. Today, Jesus invites us to find an appropriate balance between these two extremes. We have a loving Father who cares for us. This Father is also an all-powerful and perfect God whom we should seek to obey.

Read aloud Luke 12:1–12 and note to whom Jesus is first speaking:

Can leaven be removed from a loaf of bread? Can it be seen within a loaf of bread?

To what does Jesus compare this leaven?

Jesus asserts that the motives of the Pharisees along with the motives of the disciples will eventually be disclosed.

Who does Jesus warn the disciples to fear?

How does He seem to contradict this warning in vv. 6–7?

According to vv. 8–12, why don't the disciples have anything to fear?

If we belong to Jesus, we have nothing to fear! Jesus warns the disciples to look within themselves and examine their true motives. If they are not pure before God, their sinfulness will be revealed, and they will be punished. But if they belong to Christ, they are protected by the Father. The first hidden sin Jesus dealt with was hypocrisy.

Next, He dealt with covetousness. Here is the definition from Webster's dictionary: greedy, acquisitive, grasping, avaricious. "Covetous" implies inordinate desire, often for another's possessions.[16]

Read aloud Luke 12:13–40.

What did the man want Jesus to do?

How did Jesus answer him?

Write out Luke 12:21.

What do you think Jesus is saying here? What would it look like to be rich toward God?

Jesus goes on to describe a man who is not rich toward God. What emotions does such a man experience? Circle all that apply:

HAPPINESS   ANXIETY   SATISFACTION

PRUDENCE   WORRY   FEAR

What does Jesus insist we must seek in verse 31?

Jesus insists that covetousness—looking at what others have and desiring it for ourselves—results in worry, anxiety, and fear. We can trust our loving Father to give us everything we need. We must allow the Holy Spirit to cleanse us from this sin in our lives. It can become a hidden motive that robs our joy and steals our focus.

Read aloud verse 32 and write out what emotions this beautiful word picture evokes from you:

Last, Jesus warns the disciples against laziness.

Read aloud Luke 12:35–40.
What does Jesus say the men must do for their master?

What will the master do for them when he returns?

Who is the master in the parable?

Read aloud Luke 12:41–48 and note what question Peter asks in verse 41:

If Jesus is the master, how were the disciples to view themselves?

If Jesus takes a long time to return, what temptation will the disciples face?

Who or what has Jesus entrusted to you? Are you managing it faithfully and with wisdom, or are you hypocritical and/or distracted by what others have?

I'm not going to lie, that last question was a tough one for me to answer. I often disparage my children for behaviors that I myself exhibit. I spend more time looking around at what other people have than I do thanking God for what He has given me. I compare my accomplishments and abilities to others, complaining that I am not as creative, crafty, culinarily skilled, clever, or cute as someone else. Then I just want to crumple in the corner and cease trying to accomplish anything—I insist any and all attempts would be better placed in someone else's hands. I get lazy. Jesus' stern words snap me back into focus. Am I pursuing the kingdom or pettily protesting the stuff of earth? The Master is returning and this majestic King of Glory is going to invite me in, sit me down at the most magnificent feast ever known, and serve me.

What in the world?

And right now, it is time for me to serve Him. He is the Master to whom we come with every care and concern. He is also the Master to whom we will give an account. Before you close your book today, sit down with Him for a few moments. Ask Him to search your heart and bring cleansing to anything that is hidden there.

Hypocrisy
Covetousness
Laziness

All hidden within, yet inviting destruction without. You have nothing to fear, dear child; bring them before your Master for forgiveness.

WEEK 5 | DAY 2

WHAT IS HIDDEN

LUKE 13

In Jesus' day, piety and religion were predominantly focused on the externals. The religious leaders performed hundreds of outward rituals to express inner purity. Without this relentless performance there was no righteousness. They walked around in fear of accidentally touching someone or something that would render them unclean. Such rigorous religiosity drifted toward an elevation of the appearance of righteousness over a reverence for God. (See Isa. 29:13; Jer. 3:10; Joel 2:12). Is it any wonder Jesus pointed out hidden sins that no one could see?

They also focused on the externals as measures of God's favor. Sickness, disease, poverty, tragedy—these were often viewed as signs of God's displeasure and punishment.

Read aloud Luke 13:1–17.

For what reason did the people believe tragedy had struck?

Instead of trying to measure others' sinfulness, what does Jesus insist they do?

What is the problem with the fig tree?

What plan do the owner of the vineyard and the vinedresser agree on?

In verses 10–17, what did Jesus do, and how did the synagogue rulers respond?

Of what sin does Jesus accuse them?

Jesus insists that the people's judgment against those upon whom tragedy had struck amounted to hypocrisy. He then warns that judgment is soon to come on all of them.

Jesus not only warned them of their impending judgment spiritually, He will soon begin prophesying of the coming destruction of the temple in Jerusalem, which happened about forty years after Jesus' death. He then demonstrates their hypocrisy by showing they care more about their animals than they do a fellow human. They will break the law to save an ox, but not a woman bound by illness.

> For additional insight regarding Jesus' references
> to Herod, the temple, and towers, see *Come to the Table*
> at www.ericawiggenhorn.com.

Was Jesus saying that all disease is from Satan? Of course not, nor should we conclude that all infirmity is directly from Satan; that would be giving him too much "credit." Jesus is playing into their false beliefs. They would never say if their cow fell into a ditch that Satan had pushed it there. He is emphasizing how it is their own hypocrisy that leads them to draw such erroneous conclusions about others' tragedies.

It is extremely important in reading parables that we don't try and over apply doctrinal principles to what Jesus is saying. Often Jesus starts with a false belief commonly held by the people of His day, puts it into a story to which they can readily relate, and attempts to open their eyes to their distorted views about God and their fellow man.

Hypocrisy—it's sin hidden inside a person's heart that can hurl waves of destruction onto those around. But there is something greater that is hidden and soon to be revealed!

Read aloud Luke 13:18–21.
To what two things does Jesus compare the kingdom of God?

We have already discussed how it is impossible to see leaven within a loaf of bread. But we can certainly see its effects. Look at the difference between a light and fluffy dinner roll and a lavash cracker. What's the difference? Leaven. I cannot dig it out. I cannot view it. But its presence is undeniable.

The mustard seed was the tiniest seed of any type of plant in Israel. It was also prolific. A wild mustard seed could take over an entire vineyard if the vinedresser didn't immediately root it out. This tiny seed falling on the soil would never have been seen by the naked eye, but its effects were monumental.

Why is Jesus contrasting these two things with the hypocrisy of Israel's religion? Jesus' yet unseen kingdom is going to overtake the unseen hypocrisy of Israel's religious leaders—its effects will be greater and more far reaching.

Read aloud Luke 13:22–35.
How does this parable demonstrate Jesus' urgency for them to repent and come into the kingdom?

What did the Pharisees tell Jesus to do and why?

How did Jesus respond?

Here we are introduced to a little foreshadowing. Did anyone else find it odd
that the Pharisees somehow were privy to a plot by Herod to kill Jesus? They
hate Herod. Since when were they part of his personal business? And why do you
suppose they wanted to remove Jesus from Jerusalem? John's gospel sheds some
additional insight as to what else had just happened.

Read John 11:38–54.
What miracle had Jesus just performed right outside of Jerusalem in the town of
Bethany?

What did Caiaphas and the rest of the religious leaders decide should be done?

Where did Jesus go as a result?

What claim did Jesus make in John 11:25?

Let's get back to Luke's gospel. For what reason did Jesus insist He must die in
Jerusalem, according to Luke 13:33–35?

What would the people say when He arrives?

There is a prophetic element to this claim—Jesus is prophesying His impending death—letting these religious leaders know that He is fully aware of their plot to kill Him and their hypocritical warnings regarding Herod. He also knows that it will happen within their holy city. But for now, He will not depart until the proper time.

Today we encountered a hidden kingdom barricaded between the hidden sin of hypocrisy and a hidden plot by Jesus' enemies. Yet this kingdom would overtake both of them, breaking them down and building anew. Sadly, we face hidden hypocrisy within our churches and a hidden plot by our enemy. But we, as members of Christ's kingdom, shall also prevail. You, dear one, serve the Resurrection and the Life. In any place and every place where the stench of judgment and death threatens to overtake you, remember Christ's promise in the wake of it: "Didn't I tell you that if you believed, you would see the glory of God?"

Do you feel the scorn of others because of a failed marriage?
A wayward child?
A lost job?
A financial setback?
A rocky relationship?
A sobering diagnosis?
Past sin?
Something else?

Right now, today, in your circumstance, the kingdom and glory of God may appear hidden. But your resurrection is coming. Just believe.

THE GOD WHO PURSUES US
LUKE 14

At this point in the gospel narrative, Jesus' teaching becomes increasingly confrontational and takes on more urgency. We're sensing the approach of a great climax. Only a few weeks remain in Jesus' ministry on earth. He is on His way back to Jerusalem for the Passover Feast and once there, He will be crucified for the sins of the world. The religious leaders who have thus far rejected Him have little opportunity left to recognize their own sinfulness and need for repentance. Likewise, the disciples have little time left to receive instruction. Jesus' miracles and parables now focus almost entirely on the hidden sins of Israel's elite. Externally they appear righteous, but internally they're filled with hypocrisy, pride, and greed.

One of their primary sins that Jesus seemed to particularly abhor was their lack of concern for those in need. Because these men were so focused on the externals, they viewed all tangible lack in another's life as an open picture of God's displeasure with them. Yet they cared for their animals and possessions meticulously. Jesus frequently pointed out the absurdity of this view by citing misfortunes of animals and how they would never attribute such accidents to the animal's culpability. (Remember Luke 13:15? See also Luke 14:5.) Yet all physical misfortune suffered by humanity somehow justified their blame toward them.

Read aloud Luke 14:1–6.
From what ailment did the man suffer?

I almost have to wonder if Luke didn't put this story in here for humorous purposes. Luke was a physician before he was an author, remember? As we make our way through Jesus' dinner conversation, we will find the mention of this particular disease strikingly illustrative. "Dropsy" is an older term for retention of water and a swelling up of the body. Here was a man "puffed up," physically receiving the healing touch of the Savior, while those around Him who sat puffed up spiritually chose to remain in their diseased state.

Read aloud Luke 14:7–24.

In what way were the guests of this banquet demonstrating pride?

Whom does Jesus specifically address in v. 12?

How do you suppose he felt about this admonition considering he had invited his friends and fellow religious elite?

In Jesus' day, initially a great banquet would be announced by a host. Like a "save the date" announcement today. At that time, those who are invited make a firm commitment to attend the event. They RSVP at the time of this announcement, and it is shameful if they do not attend once the banquet is prepared.

When the announcement was given that the banquet was ready, what excuses were given for their lack of attendance?

With what emotion did the master respond?

What did he tell his servant to do?

When there was still room at the banquet, what did the master tell the servant to do next?

The excuses offered by these guests are ridiculous. It would be like me saying, "I'm sorry, I just bought a home off the internet across town and now that I have paid two hundred thousand dollars for it, I should probably drive over there tonight and take a look at it. I can't come to your party after all." No one in Jesus' day would buy a field or five oxen without first examining them. Anyone who did that would be considered out of their mind. Likewise, marriages were planned months in advance. To suddenly be married after the initial invite would be highly un-likely. Jesus is emphasizing that their rejection of the master's invitation is conde-scending and nonsensical. To give such excuses is to publicly shame and humiliate the host.

However, even though the master is angry at them for their shameful rejection, he does not retaliate. Instead he extends invites to those who would not normally be invited. In Jewish culture, one generally invited their social peers to their home for dinner, not those whom they did not normally engage with in society. A broad modern-day equivalent could be, "Offer hospitality to those who cannot recipro-cate or repay." A specific example might be a business owner graciously opening their home to employees or a college professor inviting their students over for a meal. There is an element not only of generosity of tangible food but the social generosity of recognizing another as your equal even though your current societal roles differ. It is a picture of Christ's kingdom: a place where we all stand equally before the shadow of the cross.

After the servant has obeyed his master and invited the poor and blind and lame, he returns letting him know there is still yet more room at his banqueting table. At this point, he tells his servant to go beyond the city itself, "to the highways and hedges," and compel even more people to attend. The parable abruptly ends before we find out if the servant followed this order and what happened as a result.

The parallels to Jesus' ministry are astounding. He frequently invited the "sinner" to dine with Him. He, too, is preparing a table as He has already told us in Luke 12. Thus far, however, He has only extended an invitation to those in the city, His fellow Jews. Not the religious Jews, but those whom the Pharisees never imagined would be included in the great messianic feast. Yet, there is still room in His kingdom. His servants will go beyond Jerusalem and Judea, beyond the confines of Israel, to invite those who are "outside the city" into the great banquet. His disciples will be the ones who complete this invitation.

How does this parable echo the prophecy of Isaiah 25:6–9?

The narrative now appears to take an unexpected turn unless we examine it closely.

Read aloud Luke 14:25–33.

What types of relationships does Jesus begin to describe (circle one):

FRIENDS   **PROFESSIONAL RELATIONS**   **FAMILY MEMBERS**   **SOCIAL CLASSES**

What does a builder do before he begins to build?

What does a king do before he wages war?

What must someone do before he or she decides to follow Jesus?

It seems to me that Jesus introduces a totally different topic here, but I think if we look at His ideas closely, we will see some striking parallels. As is the case today, banquet or dinner invitations generally centered around relationships. Religious leaders invited religious leaders. Tax collectors invited tax collectors. The wealthy invited the rich. But Jesus' kingdom banquet crosses these social boundaries.

Even more binding than these religious and economic classes were family ties. Jesus' kingdom banquet breaks through these bonds as well. Finally, entrance into this banquet is open to anyone, no matter your family, religious fervor, or social class. It is a generous invite from a host who knows you cannot ever repay Him. However, acceptance of Jesus' invitation implies a certain expectation from Him— He expects your firm commitment and resolve to show up.

In Jesus' day, when rabbis taught they would often begin their points with explanations such as, "On the one hand," and then finish their point. And afterward, they would take the opposite approach, "While on the other hand," and present a counterargument. In essence, this is what Jesus is doing here. On the one hand, He offers an invitation to all to come feast in His kingdom. On the other hand, before you accept His invitation, consider how firm you are in your commitment to attend.

Read aloud Luke 14:34–35.
What happens to un-salty salt?

We have to picture the scene. They are all lying around a table eating sumptuous fare while Jesus delivers harsh admonitions. First, He shames them for their hypocrisy by healing a man whose body is swelled up. Then He confronts the prideful guests who haughtily chose seats of honor. Next, He suggests that the host of the meal would have been more pious if he had invited the poor and the blind and the lame rather than his rich and religious friends. So far Jesus has not exactly been a congenial dinner guest.

In contrast, He presents Himself as such a host who is shamed by the community for His generosity. After all of this He makes an outrageous claim that He has the authority to demand the strictest considerations of those who would seek to follow Him. Then suddenly, as if while gazing at the food before them, or picking up a piece of leftovers, He makes this comment about salt.

What's interesting is that the only way salt can lose its saltiness is from overexposure to water. It's as if He is saying, "Can you imagine if we ate this meal and none of it were salted?" Salt preserved and brought flavor to the food. Jesus is implying that those around the table with Him had lost their saltiness. They had been puffed up and overexposed to water. (Remember the man's disease at the beginning of the meal?) In other words, they brought nothing of value to God's kingdom—they were waterlogged. He wasn't exactly offering compliments to the chef.

Jesus offers each of us an invitation into His kingdom. By believing that His death and resurrection paid for our sins, and RSVPing to His divine invitation to follow Him, He offers us a seat at His table. Have you answered His invitation, or have you offered excuses as to why you cannot come? For an explanation of God's great plan of salvation, see page 99.

Who first shared with you Christ's generous offer to come to His banquet and be part of His kingdom? What compelled you to come to Christ?

Have you thought about our Master's call to go out and compel others to join us in accepting His invitation? Who among your friends and acquaintances needs to know they have been offered a seat at Christ's table?

There is plenty of room. Won't you come? And be sure to bring a friend.

WEEK 5 | DAY 4
THE GOD WHO PURSUES US
LUKE 15

Isn't it amazing how dour some Christians can be? We serve a King who regularly went to dinner parties! The religious leaders of Jesus' day perpetually complained how often Jesus ate and drank with "sinners." Jesus is saying, "It's time to celebrate! The kingdom has come! The way of peace is being offered!" But the religious leaders would have no part of it.

Today, Jesus retells three different party scenes. What we need to focus on predominantly is what these parties tell us about God. As our eyes become unveiled to see God's heart and goodness, we are also invited to view ourselves. Where do we fit in as party guests in these stories Jesus tells?

Read aloud Luke 15:1–7.

Who specifically does Jesus address in this parable?

What is lost?

What does the shepherd do?

What happens in heaven?

It would be highly unlikely that one shepherd would tend a hundred sheep alone. Anyone who owned a hundred sheep would have been considered very wealthy and would hire two or three shepherds to tend to them. Within this context, we can understand that the sheep would remain with the other shepherd, while one went off to search for the missing sheep. This statement is insulting to the Pharisees, because the insinuation is that the shepherd has lost the sheep—he is negligent in his shepherding.

A lost sheep will most likely lie down helplessly, refusing to move. Once the shepherd finds it, he will need to pick it up and place it on his shoulders, carrying it back to the community. Notice how in Jesus' parable, the shepherd bears the burden of carrying the sheep on his shoulders with joy. (Not too much longer, and Jesus will bear a cross across His shoulders to bring us into fellowship with God!)

Jesus does not end the parable with the shepherd simply locating the sheep. The crescendo of the story is the celebration among the community that the sheep has been brought back. Jesus is implying that these lost sheep of Israel, to whom the Pharisees refer as sinners, belong to the Shepherd, and that God bears the burden of their restoration with joy. God delights in the search and rescue of His sheep! Can you see the parallels Jesus is making among this parable and his own mission and celebratory gatherings?

The predominant point of the parable is not the rejoicing at the end; it is in the middle of the parable, which emphasizes God's great joy in going out to search for His sheep and carrying them back to the fold.[17] The focus is on the great depth of divine love. The Father feels great joy in the restoration of even one sole sheep; though He may have nearly one hundred in His fold, He values each and every sheep and notices them missing. Jesus closes with irony referring to the ninety-nine who do not need to repent. This is not a theological statement—it is meant to be ironic. Sadly, there are Talmudic writings referring to rabbis who needed not to repent because they were sinless.[18] Jesus is not affirming this belief, He is disparaging it. God does not take great joy in the proposed righteousness of the Pharisees, but rather in the work of restoration of the sinful. Jesus is

attempting to open their eyes to the heart of God and His delight in the restoration of the sinner.

Jesus goes on to illustrate another aspect of redemption in His next parable.

Read aloud Luke 15:8–10.
What is lost?

What does the woman do?

What happens in heaven?

In this succeeding parable, Jesus uses a woman to highlight the Pharisaic attitudes
toward others: they viewed themselves as superior to the common people, to shepherds, and to women. Jesus uses these three groups to illustrate moral virtue, while
rebuking the Pharisees for their self-righteousness.

The idea of community is again highlighted in this parable. Some scholars suggest
this coin could have represented her dowry, which would remove her from regular
community life by rendering her unable to marry. Jesus is emphasizing that these
groups of people who are currently despised by the Pharisees are loved by God and
invited to be restored into the community. Jesus welcomes them into His kingdom
and rejoices when they repent.

Another commonly held belief among the Jews entailed the connection between
earth and heaven. "The two halves of God's creation were meant to fit together
and be in harmony with each other. If you discover what's going on in heaven,

you'll discover how things were meant to be on earth. That, after all, is the point of praying that God's kingdom will come 'on earth as it is in heaven.'"[19] Jesus' point: if heaven is rejoicing that so many are entering the kingdom, then we on earth should also.

Read aloud Luke 15:11–32.
Who leaves and comes back?

Who gets angry and complains that he has never disobeyed (which is the claim of the Pharisees to whom Jesus is speaking, by the way)?

Who behaves graciously the entire time?

What's so interesting in this parable is that we are only told of the father's reaction. Does the older brother end up forgiving him or not? Do they ever reconcile? Does the community ever accept him back, or does he continue to be the subject of gossip and judgment? Jesus doesn't tell us. He leaves us hanging on the edge of our seats in wonder.

Maybe that's because we are supposed to answer those questions for ourselves before our own gracious and forgiving Father.

Of all of the party guests in today's parables, put a star next to the ones which you can relate to and tell why:

The shepherd:

The lost sheep:

The woman:

The father:

The younger son:

The older brother:

The community:

We're all invited to this party called life. And we can all relate to one or possibly many of the guests Jesus described. Jesus invites us to rejoice that we have a Father who pursues us. He seeks us out. He rejoices in carrying us into fellowship with Him. He invites us to rejoice with others when they have been restored. He searches, watches, and waits for us to return home to Him when He has allowed us to wander off to discover just how lost we are without His presence in our lives.

And we can come enjoy the party, or we can stand outside and resent His goodness to those who seem unworthy of such lavish grace.

How will you finish the story of Luke 15? Will you come into the party and celebrate, or will you stand outside and complain that life is unfair?

Your seat at the table is waiting. Won't you come?

FAITH AND GRATITUDE

LUKE 16

Yesterday, Jesus' teaching focused on the Pharisees and religious leaders. Today, Jesus will admonish His disciples. To all who encounter Jesus on the dusty roads of Israel, a choice to reject or follow Him must be made, and quickly.

Read aloud Luke 16:1–13.

What news was delivered to the rich man?

What did the master decide to do in response to this news?

What did the manager decide to do?

A manager or a steward was a common position in Jesus' day. Typically, at harvest time, the renter would pay the landowner a certain amount of his crop per his rental contract. The manager would also receive a certain cut, off the record. It is not yet harvest time, but the manager summons the renters and greatly reduces their debt, leading the renters to believe that this generous reduction is an agreement he has convinced the landowner to allow. The steward could conceivably advocate for the renters, as he was the one present on the rented land. He would have known if there had been little rain, unexpected pestilence, a hotter-than-normal summer, anything that could have caused the land to be less productive.

Consider this contemporary comparison: "The steward thus achieves the position of a factory foreman who has arranged a generous Christmas bonus for all the workers. The bonus itself is from the owners. But the foreman is praised for having talked the owners into granting it."[20]

So, before the renters discover that the manager has been ousted from his position, he brings them in, one by one, has them rewrite their debt amount due at harvest time, and positions himself as a hero. Once the master discovers what the manager has done, he has two options. He can call the renters back in and tell them this was all a mistake and add the debt back onto their contract, or he can keep silent, and remain a highly esteemed master who lavishly issues grace to his renters.

So, what does this have to do with the disciples? They need to remember that they serve a kind and benevolent Master. The manager banked his ruse on this fact. If the master were harsh and vindictive, the risk would have been too great. "In a backhanded way the actions of the steward are a compliment to the master. The steward knew the master was generous and merciful. He risked everything on this aspect of his master's nature. He won. Because the master was indeed generous and merciful, he chose to pay the full price for his steward's salvation."[21]

What's Jesus' point? If a dishonest manager can rely on the mercy of a kind and benevolent master to care for him, how much more can Jesus' disciples rely on God?

The focus of the story isn't on the behavior of the manager, it's on the mercy of the master. Jesus is warning His disciples that they are going to face difficulty. They will be stripped of possessions and position, just like the manager. They will be placed in great crises of self-preservation to carry out the work of the kingdom. But they have a benevolent Master. He will care for them. He will give them what they need—and sometimes in ways they might not expect. The Master is asking them to remain faithful and trust in His goodness. They have a position in Christ's kingdom and possessions awaiting them in heaven they cannot fathom. They must not become distracted by a pursuit of earthly gain.

Read aloud Luke 16:14–17.

How did the Pharisees respond to this story?

How did Jesus answer them?

What might be some examples of things that our world exalts but God abhors?

Write out verse 17:

Remember when the manager reduced the debt of the renters? Changing the numbers needed only one dot, or the least stroke of a pen. Jesus boldly claims that the Master has mercifully reduced the debt to achieve righteousness. He has offered salvation to the managers—the religious elite who had been put in place to manage God's sacred land of Israel—but Jesus says they will refuse His generosity. Heaven and earth would have to pass away before they would accept His benevolence on their behalf. They had been unfaithful in their management.

What issue does Jesus address in Luke 16:18?

This seems a bit randomly thrown in here, but I think Jesus is going back to the mismanagement by the Pharisees in contrast to the mercy of the master. In Jesus' day, many rabbis taught divorce was philosophically against God's law, yet practically, men could divorce their wives for something as simple as disliking her cooking. (I'd be toast in that culture!) Jesus is highlighting a glaring example of their gross mismanagement of God's laws by citing the horrible predicament these teachers of the Law rendered to women who had no way to support themselves apart from a husband. These "managers" did not reflect the kindness and generosity of the master. But Jesus is not finished.

Read aloud Luke 16:19–31.

Who are the two people Jesus mentions at the beginning of the story?

What happens to each of them after they die?

When Lazarus is unable to comfort the rich man with even a drop of water, what does he implore Abraham to send Lazarus to do?

How does Abraham respond?

Again, this isn't a doctrinal story about what happens when people die. It's not a promise that people's lots in heaven will be counter to their fortunes on earth. It's not a story to use as proof that people from the dead can come back and walk the earth. It's also not declaring that Abraham holds the authority to determine who is in heaven and hell. The religious leaders of Jesus' day who espoused the doctrine of a final resurrection described admittance into the afterlife as "going to Abraham's bosom." Again, Jesus is taking commonly held beliefs and putting them into a story to demonstrate a point.

Jesus is restating what He had said back in verse 17: heaven and earth would have to pass away for these rich religious rulers to come to repentance. The Law and the prophets have been sent. He Himself will soon die and come back to life, and yet these spiritual elite will still not recognize Jesus' way toward righteousness. He is warning them that they will face spiritual judgment for their self-righteousness, hypocrisy, and greed.

These who oppose Jesus now will oppose the disciples. They will imprison Peter and John and behead James. The disciples will soon face physical, along with spiritual, opposition in the same way Jesus will once they arrive in Jerusalem. Following Jesus will cost them their very lives. They live among the sons of darkness. Therefore, they must remember the kindness and benevolence of their Master. He will care for them—they need not fear. They need only to trust the Master.

Do you have an area of your life in which you are struggling to remain faithful?

Your schoolwork?
A marriage?
Parenting your children?
Performing your job/ministry with excellence?
Caring for aging parents?

How would pausing to focus on the kindness and benevolence of your Master, even in light of your failings, change your perspective?

We can count on His goodness. We need only to remain faithful.

unexplainable
INVITATIONS

THE COMING KINGDOM

LUKE 17:11–37

We have already discussed back in Luke 7 the relationship between faith and healing. In that account, no faith was exhibited by the one being healed. In today's story, the opposite is true. It was not until the ten lepers stepped out in faith that they began to experience their healing. So, which premise is true: Healing requires faith? Or faith is not required for healing to occur? I would suggest both are true because each instance of healing is personal. And, more importantly, we cannot put God's plans and premises for healing into a box that we can examine and manipulate.

The moment I can put God into a box of my own logic and reasoning, predicting everything He will and won't do and why, is the moment I have made Him too small. His purposes are often beyond our reasoning. We cannot say He healed because we had faith, nor can we say that if we have faith, He must heal. Neither can we say He didn't heal because of lack of faith or that where faith is absent, His healing power is limited.

People cannot control God's actions either positively or negatively. He is sovereign in all His ways. God can, however, require steps of faith and/or obedience from us before He decides to work on our behalf.

Read aloud Luke 17:11–19.

Who did Jesus encounter on His way to Jerusalem?

By what title did they address Jesus?

When and how did their healing occur?

Who was the only one who returned to praise God?

To what did Jesus attribute the man's cleansing?

When an Israelite had leprosy, they would have to present themselves to the priests to be declared clean and thus able to reenter the community. "Leprosy" was a term used for contagious skin diseases that required isolation of the sufferer of the disease to limit its spread. When these men departed from Jesus, they still had leprosy. In faith, they left Jesus' presence believing that by the time they reached Jerusalem, their leprosy would be gone and the priest would declare them clean. The healing occurred after they exercised faith.

Interestingly, the term "Master" has several uses in Greek, none of which would be equivalent to "Messiah, Christ, or Lord," but rather a person of high standing.[22] It was a term of respect, not of worship, yet the Samaritan alone returned, attributing his healing to the power of God working through Jesus. We have previously mentioned that there was no cure for leprosy in Jesus' day. Their only hope was a miracle from God.

Have you ever been in a situation in which your only hope is a miracle from God? Sometimes those hopeless situations bring us to our knees begging God for mercy like the lepers. Other times those situations have left me in a puddle on the floor barely able to breathe. I find it so interesting that these lepers had faith in Jesus to heal them even though they did not fully understand who He was. Maybe Jesus' expectation in having them exercise some faith to experience their healing was meant to trigger within them the most important question of all: In whom exactly are you putting your faith to heal you?

I don't know about you, but my problem most often isn't that I don't have faith. It's that I don't have faith in the greatness of my God. I have made Him too small. I've relegated Him to a Master instead of the majestic, magnificent Almighty. Could it be that when Jesus asks us to exercise faith before He steps in and works, He is asking us to remember the greatness of the One in whom our faith lies?

Read aloud Luke 17:20–37.
What question did the Pharisees ask of Jesus?

Fill in verse 21:
The kingdom of God is _____ of you.

According to verse 22, what would the disciples desire to see?

What must the Son of Man experience before He would be seen by all?

To what two events in Israel's history does Jesus compare His return?

What will happen to those who seek to save their own lives?

Does this narrative sound more like a glorious celebration or a foreboding warning? How so?

Jesus is also on His way to Jerusalem and offering an invitation to take hold of the healing that will be offered there through His suffering, death, and resurrection.

In this passage, Jesus is predicting His death and the disciples' desire to see Him again as they did during the days when He walked among them. After His death, resurrection, and ascension, judgment is going to occur. Just as in the days of Noah and Lot, no one knows when this judgment will begin, but they should expect it and be ready. When it comes, they must flee immediately. The word for vultures is the same word for eagles in the Greek. Some scholars believe this is a cryptic reference to Roman soldiers who bore Rome's emblem of an eagle upon their uniforms and that Jesus is prophesying against the impending destruction of Israel. Other scholars assert this prophecy refers to an end-time judgment, when Jesus returns to earth to judge it.

The most important question for you and me, dear one, is will we face judgment from Jesus, or the welcoming arms of the One in whom we have placed our faith for forgiveness? Will you and I, like the lepers, rise up and walk in faith that our full cleansing is coming?

While we may continue to make well-educated scholarly guesses as to how the events of Jesus' return precisely unfold, He leaves no doubt about how we secure ourselves against God's judgment: we must put our faith in this unexplainable Jesus and His payment for our sin through His death on the cross and our promise of new life through His resurrection.

So, let's get practical with our own lives for a moment. You have been issued an invitation to take your place in God's kingdom plans. Are you sitting back insisting you need greater faith to rise up and take your place? Jesus told the lepers to "Go and show yourselves." He further stated that the power of the kingdom is "within our midst." Have we laid hold of it? These stories are invitations to action.

In both accounts, immediate response is expected. We can sit around and believe our circumstances to be hopeless. We can continue to sit on the side of the road, refusing to get up and move until we visually see tangible evidence of God's healing power in our lives, or we can "go and show" the world the great God in whom we have put our faith. We can mentally search the Scriptures hoping for our faith to be increased, doubting our ability to make an impact until God tangibly assures us we are ready. Or we can rise up and begin to walk in faith.

What situation are you currently facing that feels like it requires great faith but in actuality it only requires a little faith in a great God?

What would moving forward in faith look like in this situation?

What would refusing to move and trying to "save your life" in this situation look like?

And just how big, exactly, is your God?

UNEXPLAINABLE PRAYER

LUKE 18:1–17

As Jesus continues to journey closer to Jerusalem, He will continually try and focus His disciples on the greatness of the God they serve. They need not fear. Jesus' words to His disciples before the greatest faith test of their lives wasn't "Don't worry! You have enough faith to carry you through!" Nor was it, "You've got this! You can do it!" Jesus did the exact opposite. He took the focus off them and put it on God. When we are facing trials, tests, or tribulation, it is on the greatness of God alone we must put our focus. As someone who frequently feels as though I continually fall short of others' expectations of me, along with my own expectations of myself, these teachings of Jesus bring me great comfort.

Read aloud Luke 18:1–8.

If an unrighteous and unjust judge is able to do what is right, what does Jesus insist His disciples can depend on the Father to do for them?

While Jesus was certain of God's character and faithfulness, of what was He uncertain?

Jesus' point is clear: if as disciples we are going to stay faithful until His return, we must focus on the character and power of God.

What are some aspects of God's character that are particularly helpful to remember in your current season and circumstances of your life?

Read aloud Luke 18:9–17.
How does Jesus insist His followers must view themselves?

How should we view one another?

How does Jesus emphasize this point even more in verse 16?

What do you think Jesus means when He says we need to receive the kingdom "like a child"?

I was talking with a friend the other day, and he was lamenting how often Christians will come to God when they are in the midst of a tragedy or a seemingly unsolvable problem, but as soon as the crisis is over, they somehow seem to forget about Him. Others try to follow God, but when life unravels, they assume God doesn't really love them or He isn't as good as they thought, and therefore abandon their faith. Jesus' stories here highlight the dangers of thinking about God in such ways. If we think God owes us something because of our own goodness or obedience, Jesus warns we will most likely lose faith. If we feel we are somehow more deserving of His blessings than others, we will also lose faith when the blessings seemingly run dry.

A child implicitly trusts his or her parent to do the right thing. So it should be with our heavenly Father. That which He withholds is for our good. That which He gives is for our good. That which He works together is always for our good. For us and for others. We must trust in His goodness. And when He gives and then asks us to give it back, in this too we must trust Him.

Do you think it is easier or harder to feel close to God when you are walking through something difficult? Why do you feel that way?

Do you tend to view difficult circumstances as a sign of God's displeasure? How do today's stories refute this idea?

In your own journey with Jesus, have difficult circumstances tested your faith, built your trust, or a little of both?

Do not lose heart, dear one. The Father hears your cries.

WEEK 6 | DAY 3
EYES TO SEE
LUKE 18:18–43

Thus far this week, Jesus has implored us to remember God's greatness, goodness, and faithfulness. Today is an invitation to ponder His worthiness, closing with an invitation to fully see Him for all that He is! Let's sit right down and look up, gazing at our great God today.

Read aloud Luke 18:18–30.

Who is talking to Jesus, and what does he want to know?

Why does Jesus question being addressed as "good"?

Which commandments does Jesus cite specifically? (See Ex. 20:1–21.)

How did the young man respond?

What challenge did Jesus elicit next?

What emotion did the young man experience in response to this challenge?

What analogy did Jesus offer to compare wealth to entrance into God's kingdom?

How did the people respond to this analogy?

How did Peter respond?

What did Jesus assert Peter would receive?

In case the disciples somehow took this promise to mean their lives were forever rosy as a result of choosing to follow Him, what warning did Jesus issue next in verses 31–34?

How did the disciples respond to this warning?

I was first introduced to this story as a freshman in college. Our professor told us to go home and read this story and return to class with our hypothesis as to what it meant. I had only been a Christian for a couple of years at this point in my life and when I read it, I too felt sad. Did following Jesus really mean I had to give up everything I owned and take a vow of poverty? That seemed so extreme in my upper middle-class southern California world. And why had I never in my life actually met a Christian who had done this if that was what Jesus meant? I was completely at a loss. To be honest, sometimes I'm still at a loss when answering the question "What exactly does Jesus call me to give up for Him?" but I hope as we unpack this interaction today, we may have an inkling of an idea.

The wealthy young man calls Jesus "good," and Jesus insists that only God is good. Jesus isn't denying His own deity; rather, He is trying to raise awareness in the youth as to who He actually is! If Jesus is God, then eternal life is found in following Him. If this young man chooses to do so, it will require forsaking his worldly comforts afforded by wealth, as following Jesus at this point literally means traveling from place to place as His disciple.

Jesus has, in effect, drawn the man's eyes to God. Notice that the commandments Jesus chooses to cite are those found later in the list of the ten. These commandments have to do with how the young ruler treats others, not how he relates to God. The challenge by Jesus to the young man could be summed up as follows: Is God worthy of all you have?

In Jewish thought, worldly wealth was a sign of God's favor. Those who were righteous were also rich. Jesus is saying it is difficult for the rich to gain entrance to the kingdom. If those who had God's favor couldn't enter, then who in the world could? No wonder the disciples were confused! Here we have another young man trusting in his own righteousness to enter the kingdom, just like the Pharisee in the temple yesterday. Jesus insists we can never be righteous enough. Because Jesus makes us righteous through His sacrifice on the cross, He is worthy of complete obedience, surrendering anything He asks of us over to Him.

Peter is feeling pretty righteous himself about now. He, after all, has left everything to follow Jesus. So he wants to know, what's in it for him? Jesus promises good things ahead. But He also warns that dark days are coming. The disciples, however, are unable to grasp these warnings issued by Jesus. Did they not grasp it because they simply preferred not to spend a whole lot of time grappling over these strange statements made by Jesus? Or did they prefer to focus on the positive promises and ignore these dire warnings?

I hate to admit this, but I can relate to the disciples here. And to the rich young ruler. I love the promises in Scripture that bring me great comfort and peace. I prefer to gloss over these difficult demands by Jesus to hand everything over to Him in complete surrender. I'd rather skip ahead to the promises and blessings. I like to focus on the benefits, the what's-in-it-for-me parts of following Jesus, rather than the costs of discipleship.

I also can relate to the disciples' misunderstanding of circumstances. I can foolishly begin to think that God's blessings in my life are a sign not only of God's pleasure with me, but my own goodness. When things don't go my way, I blame myself, insisting that I must be disobedient in some way. It doesn't usually take long to determine where and how I am falling short in comparison to Christ's righteousness. But I also can become pharisaical and apply these same attitudes toward others. When someone's kids are rebellious, I wonder if there is some kind of sin in the home that no one knows about. Or if someone is facing financial difficulty, is it because they have made irresponsible or foolish decisions with their money? Or if someone faces a sudden and difficult medical diagnosis, is God trying to get their attention somehow? We can imagine Jesus responding with, "No, no, no! I have never called My followers to look at others' outward circumstances or even their own. I've commanded them to look at ME!"

As Jesus' followers, we will be called to give up things for His sake. It is part of the cost of following Him. Is He worthy of our surrender or not? But what Jesus promises is that what He gives us in return will far outweigh anything He ever asks of us.

Read aloud Luke 18:35–43.

What question did Jesus ask the blind man?

What do you suppose Jesus' purpose was in asking the man to articulate his desires before Him?

What did he do in response to Jesus?

Let's pause here for a moment before we close our books and allow the Holy Spirit to search our hearts.

Is there something you sense Jesus is asking you to surrender to Him today?

Imagine Jesus standing before you today and asking you, "What do you want Me to do for you?" How would you respond?

If your request was granted, would you follow Jesus unconditionally as the blind man did, glorifying God?

This unexplainable Jesus stands before you today and says, "Follow Me!" He is worthy of all that He asks of us. He is generous to give beyond what we could ever ask or imagine. When Jesus pries open our hands, we can walk sadly away, or we can glorify God knowing He has plans to place within our palms something that will bring us more joy than anything the world could ever offer.

GIVING AND GIVING BACK

LUKE 19:1–27

Yesterday, I mentioned the challenge by my college professor to read Luke 18 and determine what Jesus meant when He told the rich young ruler to sell all his possessions and give them to the poor. Was that a command specifically given for him, or did Jesus demand that of all His followers? Today's story sheds additional light on this question as we encounter another very wealthy fellow. Unlike the rich young ruler, this man does not reject Jesus' offer to follow Him, but wholeheartedly welcomes Jesus into his home.

Read aloud Luke 19:1–10.

What did Zacchaeus do for a living?

Where did Jesus find Zacchaeus, and what did He say to him?

How did the people respond to Jesus' lunch plans?

How much of his possessions did Zacchaeus give away?

How did Jesus respond to this?

Zacchaeus did not give away all his possessions, but he behaved generously. He valued Jesus over his possessions, and Jesus commended him. In the parable Jesus tells next, I believe He is turning the tables. Instead of discussing the difficulty of being wealthy and one's ability to humbly receive God's kingdom invitation, Jesus will highlight the possible attitude of one who has been given little means in this life.

Read aloud Luke 19:11–27.

What city was Jesus near, and what were the people therefore assuming?

In Jesus' story, how did the citizens respond to their new king in his distant country?

What did the king give to his first servant? What did he do with it?

How did the king respond?

What did the king give to his second servant, and what did he do with it?

How did the king respond?

According to the last servant, what aspect of the king's character led him to behave as he did?

How did the king respond to this characterization of himself?

What did the king do with the man's mina?

How did the people respond to this action by the king?

And what happened to the people of the kingdom he had been given to rule?

Jesus has used a rabbinic teaching style called "from the light to the heavy" three times in the last several chapters in relationship to our possessions.

Look up the following verses and fill in the blanks. I have used the ESV.

Luke 17:33: Whoever seeks to _____will lose it, but whoever loses his life will keep it. (Remember, Jesus is talking about returning to grab one's possessions rather than forsaking them to flee from judgment.)

Luke 18:14: For everyone who _____ will be humbled, but the one who humbles himself will be exalted. (The Pharisee despised the wealthy tax collector because he had gained his riches dishonestly.)

Luke 19:26: I tell you that to everyone who has, _____ _____, but from the one who has not, even what he has will be taken away. (There is responsibility with worldly wealth to keep a proper view as to whom it actually belongs and to use it wisely.)

Based on Jesus' words "whoever" and "everyone," to whom do these truths apply according to Him?

What do you notice about the circumstances of wealth in each instance?

Why would someone who has very little means, such as the servant with one mina, be tempted to view God as harsh or unfair?

According to Jesus, how does God respond to such an assessment of His character?

How does Zacchaeus's generosity demonstrate that He recognized Jesus' right to his possessions?

In what ways can we "put our minas to work" for our King and His kingdom?

How does our view of our King affect the way we handle our worldly wealth?

When we look at these passages as a whole in regard to our worldly wealth, I don't think there is a one-size-fits-all commandment in regard to what we are to do with it. Rather, I think there are warnings and admonishments about our attitude toward our resources and our view of ourselves because of what we have. The person with worldly wealth ought not to think of themselves more highly than the one who has not been given it. Likewise, the one who has been given little ought not to think of God more harshly than the one who has been given much. All possessions belong to God. How, when, and to whom they are disbursed are His sovereign decision. But from the one who has been given much, much will be expected.

Write out Romans 11:36:

All things. All things are from Him. All things belong to Him. What He asks us to give, He replaces with more. We cannot outgive God. Ever. He is worthy of all. Jesus finishes up this series of teachings demanding an answer from each of us. Who am I? and Will you follow me? If we respond as Peter with an emphatic, "You are the Christ! The Son of the Living God!" then does that not result in Peter's second response: "We have left everything to follow you!"?

What do you need to give over to Him today?

WEEK 6 | DAY 5

TRIUMPH BEFORE TRAGEDY

LUKE 19:28–48

The rest of Luke's gospel centers on the final week of Jesus' life within the city of Jerusalem. Before we enter the city gates, however, Luke implored us as readers to make our own decisions about Jesus.

Is He God in the flesh, the Lamb of God, come to save the world?

Should He hold complete authority over everything in my life, including my possessions?

For some of us, we may still not be 100 percent sure how to answer those questions. Or maybe we can answer them hypothetically or conceptually, but we are still uncertain how to live out our answers practically. As we close this week, we are going to examine Jesus as a triumphal King. We are going to see His heart toward those over whom He rules. What does He long for from His people? And maybe answering some of these questions will enable us to more confidently answer the ones above as well.

Read aloud Luke 19:28–40, and write out verse 28 below.

From which place did He issue a command to two of His disciples to go ahead of Him?

What did He tell them to do?

What question did the owners of the colt ask, and how had Jesus told the disciples to respond?

How exactly did Jesus enter the city? What were the people doing as Jesus passed by?

Based on the comments in verse 37, how large do you presume His crowd of disciples to be?

What were the disciples saying?

How did the Pharisees respond?

What was Jesus' answer to them?

What additional insight about this event are we given in Matthew 21:8–9?

Today we celebrate this event on Palm Sunday. I want to discuss this scene in greater detail so its beauty is not swallowed up in familiarity. First of all, when you stand on Olivet, or the Mount of Olives, you are overlooking the entire city of

Jerusalem, with the temple in closest proximity to you through the Eastern Gate. Jesus pausing the festive throng in this place to issue the order to retrieve the colt or donkey holds great symbolism for both the Greeks and the Jews.

What prophecy is given in Zechariah 9:9?

When the people are crying "Hosanna!" the literal meaning is "Save now!" How does the prophecy of Isaiah 62:11 demonstrate that the people are referring to Jesus as the Lord's promised one?

How are the people echoing Psalm 118:25–27 in both their words and actions? (Psalm 118 is a messianic psalm that people regularly sang on their trek to Jerusalem. It spoke of the promises of the Messianic Age.)

In Luke 13:35, what had Jesus said would happen the next time He returned to Jerusalem?

According to Ezekiel 10:18–19, which direction (north, south, east, or west) did God go when His glory departed from the temple?

According to Zechariah 14:4, from which place would He return?

In this scene Jesus is fulfilling so many prophecies given in God's Word! The Jews believed that since God's glory had departed from the temple and exited out the East Gate of Jerusalem, His glory would return in the same way when Messiah came. He would stand on the Mount of Olives and descend into the city through the Eastern Gate. This is precisely the path Jesus took coming from Jericho. Under the Romans, a conquering war hero would ride in on a magnificent warhorse. History has preserved an example of such a procession in the Arch of Titus. Consistently throughout his gospel, Luke has contrasted Jesus with the current world powers, namely Caesar, Herod, and the religious elite. The word used here in Luke's gospel can mean either colt or donkey. By purposefully using a word with double meaning, he also presents Jesus as a king fulfilling the ancient prophecy in Zechariah. The difference, however, is that the Romans rode in on a warhorse, constituting power and authority; Jesus rode in on a colt, or young horse, symbolizing peace.[23]

The crowds throwing their coats down upon the road symbolized Jesus' kingship. When a new king was crowned in Israel, this is what the people did to demonstrate their subservience to his rule. (See 2 Kings 9:13.)

This section of Jerusalem is presently under Islamic control. They have sealed up this Eastern Gate. The path from the Mount of Olives to the Eastern Gate is now a graveyard. Therefore, anyone who passed through it would be rendered unclean according to Levitical law and unable to enter the temple. Somehow, I don't think Jesus will be deterred by some mortar, concrete, or corpses.

> For a modern-day picture of the Mount of Olives overlooking Jerusalem, visit *Come to the Table* at www.ericawiggenhorn.com.

The people are claiming Jesus as their king and the Pharisees are telling Him to make them stop. Jesus' answer implies not only that He is king of Israel, but King over all creation. It also implies that this is God's plan that has been set in motion and unable to be thwarted.

According to Habakkuk 2:10–11, what had the owner of the house done causing the stone of his house to cry out for justice?

According to Luke 19:41–44, what was going to happen to the city of Jerusalem, and how did Jesus feel about it?

He was coming offering peace, but they would reject Him and suffer destruction. Jesus weeping over this means that it is as good as done. There is no turning back now. Their judgment is certain.

Read aloud Luke 19:45–48.
After Jesus passed through the Eastern Gate of the city, where did He go?

In calling the temple a house of prayer, we understand that to mean a place of intimacy and relationship between God and all people.

According to Jeremiah 7:1–15, what was God going to do to His house because His people had made it a den of robbers?

During Jeremiah's time, the temple had been destroyed by the Babylonians under King Nebuchadnezzar. Jesus is implying that another destruction of the temple is going to occur.

Look carefully at Jeremiah 7:6.

What were they about to do within the city in crucifying Christ?

The people in Jesus' day longed for a king who would destroy their enemies. They wanted to see the Romans cast down and conquered, rendering Israel an independent state. Instead, the Romans would destroy them. God had planned from the beginning for the Gentiles to experience His salvation along with the chosen people of Israel: Behold your king is coming, He comes in humility and in peace, with works of love, desiring to restore relationship among the people of earth with their God.

Can the One who came to redeem the world from sin and death also redeem us from ourselves? Do we desire restoration with God? Jesus came offering the way of peace. Will we follow Him, or choose our own path? These are the deeper questions Luke is asking us to answer about Jesus.

What would it mean today, right now, in this exact moment, to surrender to Him?

What would it mean to surrender your relationships over to Him?

Your dreams/goals/aspirations?

Your possessions?

Behold, your King is coming. Will you lay yourself down at His feet?

unexplainable
CONFRONTATIONS

WEEK 7 | DAY 1
THE GOD OF THE LIVING
LUKE 20:27-40

Jesus has now entered Jerusalem. It is His final week on earth, and He is about to perform the greatest act of love in human history. He will be put on trial as a sinless, innocent man, be condemned to death and then raised to life as the Son of God. Jesus has kindled the ire of religious leaders to a whole new level after His claims of authority within the temple by turning over the tables. These leaders have plotted to kill Jesus; now they lie in wait to trap Him in His words or actions. Today, we will see the religious elite attempting to divide Jesus' popular support by asking Him yet another question. I also think they were fishing for Jesus to divulge some additional information about His personal resurrection claims, hoping to trap Him.

Read aloud Luke 20:27-33.

According to Luke 20:34–36, whose wife would this widow be after the resurrection?

How did Jesus explain in Luke 20:37–38 that even Moses had proven the resurrection?

We know the Sadducees accepted the written Law, the writing of Moses, which comprise the first five books of the Bible. They did not, however, believe in the resurrection of the dead. It is brilliant, then, that Jesus draws His argument for the resurrection from the writing of Moses.

How did the scribes respond to Jesus' answer in Luke 20:39?

What did they resign themselves to no longer attempt in Luke 20:40?

Write out Luke 20:38 here:

Underline that last phrase: "for all live to him."

I love how the New International Version states it: "For to him all are alive."

Let's take that apart a little more closely. What is Jesus actually saying there? We have to remember that this current encounter is depicted as a direct challenge to Jesus' authority. He has claimed authority over the temple, which was held by the chief priests and ultimately the High Priest. They challenged His authority over Caesar by asking Him a question about paying taxes. They are now challenging Jesus' authority over the afterlife, the final resurrection believed by the Pharisees to come during the Messianic Age (even though the Sadducees don't even acknowledge a final resurrection!). If Jesus claims authority over this resurrection, His audience would have understood Him to have been making a divine claim in doing so. This is why we need to get to the root of Jesus' answer: Does He claim authority over this final resurrection or not?

So far, Jesus had dodged both direct confrontations about His claims to authority. He refuses to answer their question regarding His authority to disrupt the temple (see vv. 1–8) and He expertly answers their question about paying taxes (see vv. 19–26). What does He do here?

When Jesus says "all *live to him*" in verse 38, He uses two Greek words. The first word for "live" is *zao* and it means to be alive, live again, or resurrection life.[24] The second word is *autos* which means "same, pertaining to that which is identical to something."[25]

Now I know that's not confusing at all, so let's put this together. Jesus is saying that in the resurrection, people will live again and have eternal life. Jesus is also making another statement that is different from their ideas about the final resurrection—according to Jesus, Abraham, Isaac, and Jacob are currently living, even though the final resurrection has yet to take place. Jesus speaks as one who has clear understanding as to what takes place in the spiritual realm. This is an incredibly bold claim on Jesus' part. Guess who the only person is who could claim to know with certainty how and when and in what regard the final resurrection takes place? Only God Himself!

What does any of this have to do with us today? Well, if we know that Jesus has ultimate authority over what is going to happen to us after we die, shouldn't that result in Him having some authority over our lives today? And if His plan is to make us like Himself after we are resurrected, how greatly are we cooperating with Him in His transformation of us today? Does He become the God of the living only after we die, or is He God over us right now—in this life?

One thing those present got right in this story: they ceased asking Jesus any more questions. I would like to get to a point in my faith journey with Jesus where I no longer seek the answers to all of my "whys." I'd like to have enough faith in His power and authority that even when things don't make sense, when I can't find a clear answer in Scripture, when it appears that there cannot possibly be a good answer, I can trust Him.

I can be certain that He knows with certainty what is happening in my life and why on earth He would allow it in light of Him preparing me to become like Him in heaven. I want to stop challenging Jesus' authority and rest in His certainty.

How about you? What are some "whys" you are currently asking Jesus?

What would it mean to begin to rest in the certainty of His authority over your circumstance or situation?

Why doesn't it make much sense to believe as a Christian that Jesus has authority over what happens to us after death, but not live in the certainty of that authority in our current, daily circumstances?

Tomorrow Jesus is going to ask a question of His own. And hopefully we'll see that, while there are things in this life that will never make a lick of sense to us, we can trust Him. He holds the power and authority to make all things right in the end. And He has a plan to do exactly that.

JESUS' QUESTION

LUKE 20:41–21:4

Understanding Jewish ideas about their Messiah could be equivalent to trying to pin down Christian concepts about end times today. The more Christians you ask, the larger variance of responses you get. Today, I'm going to throw a whole bunch of messianic cards on the table, and as we shuffle through them, we should be able to put together a hand we can play with—at least one that gives us an idea of Jesus' game plan in posing the important question He asks today.

What question does Jesus ask the Sadducees in Luke 20:41?

Why might this be difficult to understand in light of the Scripture Jesus quotes in verses 42–43?

The Jews of Jesus' day not only hotly debated the existence of an end-time resurrection, they also debated when the Messiah would come. Some believed it to be a set time appointed by God and unalterable, while others believed it was dependent on Israel's repentance. Still others believed there would not be only one Messiah, but two!

Another topic of debate was whether or not a period of judgment and calamity would occur before the Messiah appeared. They further disputed whether their current subjugation under Rome sufficed as God's judgment or if times must yet worsen.

Another point of debate was the return of David. Many Jews believed that King David would be literally resurrected from the dead and sit on the throne in Jerusalem. Others viewed this passage as a figurative depiction for the Messiah. The pious anticipated the Messiah returning the people to righteousness and a devout following of the Mosaic law. Others anticipated the political reform Messiah would bring.

Those Jews who held political power and wealth under the current system feared the consequences of a messianic revolution. In other words, there were religious and political factions in first-century Israel just as there are in our twenty-first-century world today. Trying to put everyone with whom Jesus interacted into the same box of belief proved impossible. One thing on which they did agree was that the Messiah would somehow be a direct descendant of David.

But since we know this conversation is currently happening between the Sadducees and Jesus, let's take that into account as we take it apart.

Read aloud Psalm 110 and record what portion Jesus quoted below:

This is a messianic psalm written by David over a thousand years before Jesus' birth. God had promised David that He would establish His throne forever, but historically David's royal lineage ended when the Babylonians crushed Israel in 586 BC. The Jews therefore believed that God would reinstate this covenant promise to David with the arrival of the Messiah. But Jesus poses an important question: how can the Messiah be David's son, yet David refers to him as Lord?

The Sadducees did not desire a messiah who would depose the Roman hold over Israel, nor were they looking for a messiah to usher in a kingdom of God in this world. As the Jewish ruling class they were wealthy, highly educated, and socially touted, so Roman subjugation wasn't so shabby for these guys. What they feared was the appearance of a false messiah (in their view, this would be all messianic claims as they did not truly anticipate a messiah) who would disrupt their social and political position. They saw religion as a moral code and a tool to keep the uneducated masses in line more than anything else.

So, Jesus' question attempts to open their eyes to His role as Messiah as much broader than merely instituting a political takeover and imputing the Mosaic law on society. He is greater than a mere earthly king, however magnificent King David had been. He is a Messiah who ushers in a kingdom of eternal righteousness, who transforms the living and the dead. For David to have referred to the Messiah as Lord meant He held divine status.

Read aloud Luke 20:45–47.

List the four things Jesus states in verses 45–46 the scribes love:

1.

2.

3.

4.

What two things do these scribes do that will result in greater condemnation?

1.

2.

Truthfully, there is nothing new under the sun. We all want to be recognized as successful, whether economically, educationally, professionally, socially, or religiously. We could deem success as the neighborhood in which we reside, the location of our office and the size of its window, the letters behind our name, or the emblem on our hood. It could be the fact that we have "good kids" who go to the "best schools" or who choose to spend the summer on a mission trip or decide to go into vocational ministry. Nobody wants to feel like a failure.

God doesn't want us to be apathetic failures either. The real question is, whose recognition are you seeking? The scribes sought the admiration of man, while Jesus insists we must seek the approval of God. Jesus inextricably tied social injustice to religious hypocrisy. Maybe it wouldn't be too much of a stretch to suggest that our own preoccupation with success, resulting in our inattention toward others' suffering, could also result in Jesus' condemnation.

We've been talking about Jesus' authority this week, so let's make this personal. This isn't really about how much one person has or doesn't have, but this is about the heart. Whose approval are you seeking? Who are you longing to please?

Of the types of things the scribes loved, which one tugs most tightly on your own heart strings?

Out of all of the religious activities in which you participate, which ones could most tempt you into religious pretense? (Circle all those that apply.)

CHURCH ATTENDANCE   TITHING/GIVING

SERVICE   ROLES/POSITIONS

FRIENDSHIPS/RELATIONSHIPS WITH   YOUR CHILDREN'S
CERTAIN CHURCH MEMBERS   SERVICE/OBEDIENCE

What did Jesus notice the widow doing in Luke 21:1–2?

How did He respond to this?

The temple treasury in Jesus' day held exorbitant riches. These scribes and others who were filled with self-importance liked to make much of their generous donations to the temple, and Jesus implies that they gave to win the approval of man. He wasn't celebrating poverty nor was He issuing a command to give to the point of destitution. Instead He is making a contrast in the hearts of the givers. This poor widow gave in faith that God would care for her; He was her provision. What little she had belonged to God.

Do you view your finances as your own hard-earned gain, or do you see your resources as belonging to God?

The beauty of today's lesson is that Jesus did not come to merely rule over us; He came to change us. His authority over our lives results in our becoming more like Him. We no longer fear the rejection of others or chase after things to try and seek others' approval. We cease concerning ourselves with the admiration of others because we can rest in the approval and acceptance of Christ.

We need not wonder if we've given enough or why we don't have more to give. Jesus has made us enough. In those areas of our lives where we struggle with comparing ourselves with others or seeking recognition from others, we can remember that it is only the Lord whose approval we need. He will put our enemy of self under His feet.

We also have a Savior and Lord who will eventually put an end to all social injustice in His kingdom, and those who suffer will do so no more. The beauty of this Savior is that He has invited us into this work today. Will we allow Jesus to rescue us from our endless preoccupation with self in order to be used to bring blessing and justice to others?

Why don't we pause today and lay bare our heart before our King?

A LOOK AHEAD

LUKE 21:5–38

As mentioned yesterday, the Jews of Jesus' day held varying views about the arrival and work of their promised Messiah. Those who did hold messianic expectations, however, agreed that the Messiah would be a descendant of David and that He would rule in Jerusalem, bringing Israel back to a proper relationship with God through their historical temple worship. But Jesus insists that His establishment of His messianic kingdom is going to look quite different.

Read aloud Luke 21:5–24.

What emotion would the disciples succumb to?

According to verses 5–6, what did Jesus say was going to happen to the temple?

What question did the disciples ask Jesus in response to this statement in verse 7?

What emotion would the disciples succumb to in verse 9?

Circle all the things that Jesus says will be signs that the end is at hand:

MANY WILL COME CLAIMING TO BE CHRIST OR HIS REPRESENTATIVE

WARS   A TIME OF PEACE   EARTHQUAKES

FAMINE/PESTILENCE   ECONOMIC PROSPERITY   COSMIC SIGNS

THE DISCIPLES WILL TAKE POSITIONS OF AUTHORITY   FAMILIES WILL DISAGREE OVER CHRIST

THE DISCIPLES WILL BE PERSECUTED   JERUSALEM WILL BE DESTROYED

What time is Jesus referring to exactly? One thing we must understand about biblical prophecy is that when prophets spoke, they would often group events categorically rather than chronologically.[26] It is also important to note that prophets always included some events that would happen within the lifetime of those to whom they prophesied. This was to fulfill the admonition of Moses in testing the prophets.

What did Moses tell the people in Deuteronomy 18:22?

In Jesus' prophecy here, there is an element to the prophecy that must come true in the audience's lifetime. That element would include several things:

- The disciples would be put on trial and persecuted, even by fellow Jews.
- The temple would be destroyed, which would happen in forty years from when Jesus spoke this prophecy.
- The Gentiles, namely the Romans, would lay siege to Jerusalem at the same time they destroyed the temple.

Read aloud Luke 21:25–38.

In the midst of all of the chaos of the world, what would the people behold?

Write out verses 32–33:

What warning did Jesus issue in verses 34–35?

How would the disciples "stay awake"? See verse 36.

How did the crowds respond to this teaching?

Oftentimes in biblical prophecy, we see aspects of the prophecy that would occur within the hearers' lifetime to authenticate the truth of the message, coupled with elements that appear to be more eschatological in nature, or referring more to events at the return of Christ. For example, concerning this passage, Charles Ryrie says of the question the disciples asked in verse 7, "There is a dual perspective in Christ's answer—the destruction of Jerusalem in AD 70 and the tribulation days just prior to His second coming. Verses 8–19 and 25–28 relate particularly to the latter time, whereas verses 20–24 refer to the former."[27]

Jesus has repeatedly warned His audiences about the impending destruction of the city of Jerusalem and the temple. The reference to Him coming on the clouds of heaven is an allusion to the prophecies given in Daniel 7.

According to Daniel 7:9–14, how does the Son of Man arrive?

What is the setting for His arrival?

Who is still given a time to live even though they have been stripped of some of their dominion?

You can dig more deeply into Daniel's prophecies in the free download-able resource *Come to the Table* at www.ericawiggenhorn.com.

This scene depicts the Messiah receiving His kingdom in the heavenly courts. The establishment of His kingdom on earth is going to occur after "a season and a time."

Read Daniel 7:23–27.
Who would initially rule over the saints of the messianic kingdom?

Jesus continually warns His followers to expect difficult times ahead. What is most fascinating to point out is that twice in these prophecies, Jesus used divine descriptors of Himself and the crowds offered no rebuttal against these claims.

Who comes on the clouds according to Nahum 1:3?

Third, Jesus claims that His words will "not pass away." In other words, they will certainly come to pass and they will be eternal, and in speaking so, Jesus is speaking as God here.[28]

What does any of it matter to us two thousand years later as His followers? In the midst of their chaotic world, Jesus issued a fourth important admonition.

Look back at Luke 21:8 and complete the following command: See that you are not _____. For many will come in my name . . .

How many have come in Jesus' name with false teaching attempting to lead His followers astray with new revelation?

Many movements and leaders claim they have come in Jesus' name. They lead many astray into a false gospel, often claiming that Jesus is only one way to salvation, rather than attest to Jesus' own words in John 14:6: "I am the way, and the truth, and the life. No one comes to the Father except through me."

What does Paul say in Galatians 1:6–9 about anyone who preaches a different gospel than one in which Christ is Lord: equal to the Father and the sole payment for our sins?

According to Luke 21:13, what does Christian persecution afford us?

What promise is given to us in Luke 21:14–15 when we are put on trial for our faith?

According to Luke 21:19, how are we to gain our lives?

In a world becoming increasingly hostile toward Christians, when the cares of this life tempt us toward the pleasures of the world for a quick escape, when the return of Christ feels far away, when everything appears out of control rather than securely under His dominion, these admonitions provide anchors in a swirling societal storm. The books have been opened and the kingdom has been issued to the rightful King. Straighten up and raise your head—our redemption is drawing nigh. This time and season will soon be over, and we will rule and reign with Him for all eternity. Not one single circumstance in your life is outside His care and control. He is coming on the clouds in power and glory. So stay awake, friend. You don't want to miss a thing!

WEEK 7 | DAY 4

BETRAYAL

LUKE 22:1–23

We've all heard the old adage "There's safety in numbers," right? The chief priests and scribes have a plot to kill Jesus. The problem, however, was that large crowds continually surrounded Jesus. These people were enraptured by His words and admired Him. He hinted at messianic claims, and even beyond that, at holding divine status, as we read yesterday. And none in the crowds seemed to squirm over this, except those who sought to kill Him.

Write out Luke 22:2:

These scribes and chief priests were very afraid the people would revolt under Jesus' command, bringing in the wrath of the Romans and the destruction of their temple. This meant the end of their power and their wealth. The people were hanging on to Jesus' every word, and one command from Him to rise up and revolt would mean war. And with the Romans as the enemy, it would certainly be a losing battle.

Read Luke 22:3–13.
When would they need to arrest Jesus?

passover

What did Jesus send Peter and John on ahead to do?

prepare passover

Based on what you know of Jesus' popularity among the people and hatred of Him by the Pharisees, why would it be important for Jesus to celebrate the Passover in a very discreet location?

Read Luke 22:14–22.

What did Jesus tell them would happen after He celebrated this Passover with them?

betrayal

This is not simply a typical meal that one celebrated annually, like when we make grandma's mashed potatoes on Christmas Eve. The Passover meal explicitly described the food to be served, the order in which it was to be presented, the prayers and blessings spoken by the host of the meal during each part, and a call to remember their deliverance out of Egypt under Moses.

The Jews also invoked supplication to God to bring their promised deliverer, the Messiah, who would deliver them again from the bondage of pagan nations. The problem was that Israel was not seeking a lamb who would protect them from the penalty of death, they were seeking a Moses figure who would facilitate God's wrath on their enemies. They missed the point.

The Jews believed that the Passover pointed toward a new deliverance: the messianic kingdom. As Israel had been delivered from her Egyptian oppression under Moses, they would again be delivered from pagan subjugation under the Messiah. Jesus spoke of the Passover being fulfilled once He was slain as the Lamb of God.

In verses 17–19, what did Jesus tell the disciples to do with the cup?

give thanks
take this
divide it

Jesus is speaking of the third cup of wine in the Passover feast. This is also called the "cup of redemption" by the Mishnah. It represented the blood of the Passover lamb.[29]

Fill in the order of events in the next part of the evening according to verse 19:

First, Jesus took bread.

Second, Jesus _____ gave thanks.

Third, Jesus _____ broke the bread.

Fourth, Jesus gave some to His disciples and said, "This is my body, which is given for you. Do this in remembrance of me."

Typically, in the Passover meal the bread was broken first, and then the host gave thanks for bread from the earth, remembering the poor who only had broken bits of bread for sustenance. They also expressed gratitude for unleavened bread, symbolizing the purity of Israel due to their observance of the Law.[30] Jesus reversed the order. He gave thanks that He Himself would soon be broken in order to bring true purity to Israel and to the world through His atoning death on the cross. As stated above, the procession and liturgy of the Passover meal was strictly observed. His disciples would have noticed Jesus veering from the celebration's usual course and presumably been jolted by it. Imagine singing the hymn "Silent Night" on Christmas Eve and suddenly the worship leader alters the words on you—the change would be hard to miss. It's easy to understand why Jesus would have wanted to suddenly grab their attention, when we read what He said next.

One more cup remained—the fourth cup of wine. What did Jesus call this fourth cup in Luke 22:20?

this cup is the new testament in my blood which is shed for you

Upon consumption of this fourth cup they would chant, "From everlasting to everlasting Thou art God, and beside Thee, we have no King, Redeemer or Savior."[31]

Look carefully at this closing chant—exactly who would the Messiah—the King, Redeemer, Savior—be?

Look carefully at Exodus 12:21–24. What exactly would the blood of the lamb provide for Israel?

protection

The word for "pass over" resembled the Egyptian word *pesh*, which became the Hebrew word *pasha*.[32] The literal meaning of the word is to "spread wings over," depicting a mother bird protecting her young and preserving them from danger.

How is this word picture similar to Jesus' words in Luke 13:34?

where your treasure is

How did God describe His new covenant with His people in Jeremiah 31:31–34? In what ways was the new covenant different from the old?

not where Lord took them out of Egypt

Who were the two parties in this covenant?

Lord and House of Israel

To what "old covenant" did God compare this new one?

law written in their hearts I shall be their God they shall be my people

How specifically would "the Law" be different in the new covenant?

In what ways does Jesus' death and resurrection allow the "Law" to be written on our hearts? (See John 14:26, 1 John 2:27 for additional insight.)

Holy Spirit   teach   bring all things to remembrance

According to John 14:1–11, 22 how confused do you think the disciples were over Jesus' words at the Passover meal?

Was Jesus surprised that one of His disciples was going to betray him? See Luke 22:21–22.

no

Read aloud Luke 22:23–24. *which one who is greatest*

Let's just pause here for a moment and think about the depth of Jesus' loneliness and despair in this moment. Jesus informed them that He is about to suffer. One of His dearest friends is going to betray Him. Rather than comforting Jesus in this moment, they all turn inwardly in self-justification and outwardly in criticism and comparison.

No one seems the least bit concerned about Jesus. They are too busy turning on one another. They are also too busy worrying about what all of Jesus' strange sayings mean for them personally. They are self-absorbed. Here is a difficult truth: when we are consumed with comparing ourselves and critiquing others—we are controlled by the sin of self. And there Jesus sits in the midst of all of their questioning.

I'm sadly aware of how greatly I resemble those disciples on the night of Passover. When Jesus' future plans and promises seem confusing or different than I had hoped or imagined, I can get pretty self-absorbed. I forget that Jesus called me to obey and serve Him and instead begin to point fingers and critique what everyone else is and is not doing. I begin to justify myself, insisting that there certainly isn't anything in my life that could constitute betrayal to Jesus. Instead, I become intent on figuring out where everyone else is falling short. And there Jesus sits, waiting for me to focus on Him—on His suffering for my sake—that I might live for Him.

I become like those of Jesus' day and begin to demand a strong and mighty Moses to deliver me from my circumstances instead of the Lamb of God who came as a sacrifice to save me from myself. I miss the point.

The truth is that we all betray Jesus. Every one of us. None of us lives fully for Him. So, the real question is, what will we choose to do *today*? Will we leave Jesus alone in His suffering, or will we rush to His side asking Him to show us how to live for Him?

WEEK 7 | DAY 5

SIFTING

LUKE 22:24–46

The criticism and comparison didn't stop as to who might be the betrayer. The tide quickly turned to a debate as to which of them ought to be considered greatest. Still self-absorption. Yet now it has escalated.

Looking back at Luke 22:23, what word describes their conversation toward one another?

who

Look at Luke 22:24, what word is now used to describe their conversation?

greatest

And so goes the comparison game. What began as comparison now leads to cut downs. The word "question" implies an examination together, seeking, asking. The word "dispute" implies an eagerness to quarrel or to involve oneself in strife. Do you sense the escalation? A little further along we see how this comparison game evolves. Self-assertion.

What did Peter claim of himself in Luke 22:33?

Lord, I am ready to go with thee, both into prison, and to death

How did Jesus respond?

deny me three times

How did Jesus describe Himself among them in verse 27?

I am among you as He that serves

Jesus is handing His kingdom over to them, this self-absorbed lot of knuckleheads who can't even get along with one another, let alone teach the rest of Jesus' followers what citizenship in His kingdom should look like.

Let's take a closer look at the way Jesus describes Satan's plan for Peter and the rest of the disciples.

What did Satan demand he be allowed to do to Peter and the rest of the disciples in verse 31?

sift you as wheat

What did Jesus pray over them?

that thy faith fail not; and when converted strengthen your brothers

What did Jesus command Peter to do when the "sifting" was finished?

Since the only "sifting of wheat" I've done lately is narrow down which loaf of bread to toss into my grocery cart, let's examine this process a bit more thoroughly. The first step would be to separate the edible grain from the chaff. This would be done manually and is a purification process. Second, the grain would be placed in a sieve. The lighter grain, along with the weevils, would fall through the sieve, while the dense, heavy grain would remain within it. The grain would be shaken and tossed within the sieve so all the lightweight pieces and the destructive insects would fall out. Further purification. It's all edible now, but the fluffy stuff gets removed.

Next, this dense grain is put in a pile, while the farmer takes a large winnowing fork and tosses the grain up into the air. Any additional lightweight pieces are blown away, while the heavy, dense grain falls back down into the pile. The farmer takes his winnowing fork to the pile several times, removing all the wheat that is not substantive.

Do you get the idea that this isn't a quick and easy process? The disciples are going to be tossed and shaken, thrown about again and again, and in the end, if their faith is not of enough substance, they shall simply be blown away.

Look carefully at Jesus' answer to Simon. How certain does He seem that the disciples will make it through this sifting process?

+

To what does He attribute their success?

His prayer for faith

The reason the disciples will pass this testing of their faith is because Jesus has prayed for them. And Jesus is also praying for you and for me (see Rom. 8:34 and Heb. 7:25). And when we make it through our own sifting process, what remains is a solid, dense, life-giving faith.

Think about what happens to that wheat. It becomes bread—solid, satisfying sustenance to a hungry world. Whenever and however our enemy has been allowed to sift and toss us, Jesus has a plan to solidify and purify us, transforming our faith into something that can offer life and sustenance to others in their own sifting circumstances. I want that kind of faith; how about you?

But the disciples aren't there yet. Jesus attempts yet again to turn their eyes back onto Him for direction.

How does Jesus' question to the disciples in verses 35–37 imply His care for them?

did not lack anything

Looking back at Luke 9:10–17, what miracle did Jesus perform right after the disciples returned the first time they were sent out?

5 loaves 2 fish food for 5,000

What did the disciples have to do that they were reluctant about in this miracle?

What is the common item in both the wheat conversation and this miracle? Bread! In the feeding of the five thousand, the crowds received the bread gratefully. The day is now coming when the people will reject Jesus as the Bread of Life. Jesus is reminding them that following Him means doing some difficult, even impossible, things.

How would the people label Jesus according to verse 37?

transgressor *must have an end*

Jesus is sternly warning them that danger is imminent. He promises they will make it through these dangerous times simply because He has prayed for them. But let's see what happens when He implores His disciples to pray for Him.

Read aloud Luke 22:39–46.
What did He ask the disciples to pray for?

pray to avoid temptation

What did Jesus pray for Himself?

remove this cup not my will but thine be done

Who came and ministered to Him?

Angel from heaven

How great was Jesus' agony in this moment?

Luke

extreme

sleeping sorrow

What did He find His disciples doing?

What about you? What temptation would you face in this <u>circumstance</u>?

The truth is that this life is going to sift us. We are going to go through some circumstances in this life that will leave us so badly shaken, we'll wonder if we can ever stand up straight again. Interview ten people in your church over fifty years of age. They will all tell you of a time or two their faith was tossed in the air and rattled by the winds of change. It's part of life on this weevil-infested fallen planet. But do you know what else these saints will tell you? Their faith became solidified. It gained some strength and some density it didn't have prior to the sifting. They'll also tell you how God used that season of being shaken to the core to bring stability to another quaking saint. It's just God's way. Every time.

And do you know what else I bet they would all say? People prayed for them. It was the prayers of the saints that grounded them when their circumstances left them reeling and searching for something to hold on to. It was prayer that pressed them into Jesus.

Matthew spirit is willing flesh is weak

Have you been sifted? Are you being sifted now? Jesus longs to take that which is weak and wily and make it into something strong and permanent. He longs to take raw wheat and make it into life-giving bread, to bring nourishment to His people. But through that transformation process we will face temptation.

It's too hard.
It's not fair.
It's taking too long.
It's more than I signed up for.

And in our weariness and despair we'll be tempted to lie down and fall asleep. But Jesus says to keep our eyes open. He has prayed for us. And when the sifting is over—and one day it surely will be—we will have turned into solid saints of strength, providing encouragement to our brothers and sisters.

AN
Unexplainable
RESCUE

THREE-RING CIRCUS

LUKE 23:1–25

My husband and I used to love to watch the television series *24* together. In fact, throughout twenty-four years of marriage, I'm pretty sure it's the only television program both of us equally enjoyed. Each episode chronologically depicted one hour in the life of the characters, and the premise was that each season, spanning nearly a year of television watching, occurred within one twenty-four-hour period. That's how it is with this portion of Luke's gospel. There is so much action crammed into one twenty-four-hour time period, we could lose sight of the intensity if we are tempted to span it out across days or months.

The Passover began on Thursday at sundown. For nearly a week now, Jesus and His disciples have been in Jerusalem, and He has been preaching daily in the temple courts. For a solid week before the day of the Passover, the Jewish people celebrated the Feast of Unleavened Bread. The two feasts became synonymous with each other and many Jews would travel to Jerusalem for both feasts.

After the Passover meal, which could have lasted as late as nine or ten p.m., the disciples headed out to the garden of Gethsemane near the Mount of Olives, which is where Jesus separated Himself to pray. While in the garden, Judas brought the temple guards to arrest Him. From there they took Him to Annas's house, the former chief priest and father-in-law of the current chief priest, Caiaphas. This gave them time to assemble enough members of the Jewish council in order to put Jesus on trial. It is now the middle of the night, somewhere between midnight and two a.m.

From there, they took Him before Caiaphas and the Sanhedrin, which was the Jewish ruling court. It is now daybreak.

Matthew 26:57–68 describes Jesus before Caiaphas and the council. What do verses 63–65 tell us Jesus said to Caiaphas that led him to tear his priestly robes?

Pilate was the Roman governor of Judea, the region in which Jerusalem was located. He only allowed trials between sunrise until before noon. It is still very early in the morning. The Jewish rulers must twist Jesus' words to have Him appear as an insurrectionist and potential threat to Rome's civil rule. If they presented Him to Pilate with the complaint that He claimed to be the God of Israel, Pilate would have laughed them out of his palace. The Jewish rulers knew they would only secure a crucifixion from their Roman governor for political reasons, not religious ones.

Read aloud Luke 23:1–5.
What three things did they accuse Jesus of doing?

How do these accusations compare with Luke 20:19–26?

What question did Pilate ask Jesus?

How did Jesus answer him?

How does Luke describe the religious leaders' response to Pilate's verdict?

Based on Luke's use of this description, how would you gauge the emotional temperature in this hearing?

What additional insight are we given in Matthew 27:15–26 that helps account for Pilate's preference to release Jesus rather than condemn Him?

What else are we told in John 19:6–8 that may have influenced Pilate's decision?

Pilate smells something fishy. His wife's cryptic warning doesn't help. We learn from extrabiblical writers such as the historian Josephus that Pilate was a cruel ruler who would maintain order using the most brutal of methods. Yet each gospel writer makes it exceedingly clear that in the case of Jesus, Pilate only reluctantly imposed his power to issue Jesus' death sentence.

Read aloud Luke 23:6–16.
What did Pilate decide to do when he discovered Jesus was from Galilee?

How did Herod respond to this idea?

What about Jesus' presence before Herod disappointed him?

Why would arraying Jesus in splendid clothing prove to be a mockery toward Christ?

Describe Pilate and Herod's relationship prior to meeting Jesus and then afterward.

What conclusion did Pilate reach after Herod returned Jesus to him?

We may have gotten through one or two episodes of *24* by now, but it is still very early in the morning. Remember, Pilate did not hold any trials past noon. Within this time period, Jesus has appeared before the Sanhedrin, appeared before Pilate, been sent over to Herod, and then returned to Pilate yet again.

Look carefully at Luke 23:13.
Who exactly is appearing before Pilate during this trial?

Read aloud Luke 23:18–25. Based on the verse above, who does "all" consist of?

I used to picture this scene involving every Jew in Jerusalem shouting before Pilate. In actuality, however, it is the Jewish rulers standing before him. The common person was probably still at home after a late evening celebrating the Passover. Most Jews may still be unaware that all of this has taken place. That makes a lot more sense to me, considering that five days ago the multitudes were ready to make Him their King.

This is not a verdict presented before large masses of crowds. This is a covert conspiracy by the Jewish leaders to deliver Jesus over to death out of envy of His popularity and fear that He might somehow convince the people to rebel, therefore stripping away their current position and power under the Romans. Jesus called this their "hour of darkness" and, while the last twenty-four hours must have felt like an eternity to Jesus, He knows this suffering will last a short time in comparison to the eternity of heaven.

According to Hebrews 12:2, what was Jesus' attitude toward the cross that awaited Him?

Dear one, I don't know what you must endure in this life. Here are but a handful of what our Savior faced:

Mockery   Shame   Abuse   Persecution

Pain   Torture   Abandonment   Betrayal

Slander   Loneliness

But this I do know: If you are a follower of Jesus, joy awaits you. Everlasting joy. Triumphant joy. Unexplainable joy. Now is the hour of darkness, but the light will come.

WEEK 8 | DAY 2
THE DARKEST HOUR
LUKE 23:26–49

It would be about this time in the morning that people would be arriving at the temple for morning prayers and sacrifices. Yet prior to 9:00 in the morning, the city would be relatively quiet at the temple mount. Upon their arrival, the people would have been struck by a most horrific sight: Jesus of Nazareth beaten, bleeding, bruised, struggling to walk, donned with a crown of thorns thrust into His skull, being led to a cross on the side of the road.

Read aloud Luke 23:26–31.

Based on all that Jesus has endured the past twenty-four hours, why do you think Simon of Cyrene was seized to carry Jesus' cross for Him?

Who is following Jesus, and what are they doing?

Again, we have yet more evidence that the crowd before Pilate did not constitute large numbers of Jewish people. The crowd screaming, "Crucify Him!" were the Jewish religious leaders. The common people now realize what is happening and are lamenting.

Which group of people did Jesus specifically address as He made His way to the site of the crucifixion?

What dire warning did He give to them?

What question did He ask them?

Why do you suppose Jesus specifically addressed the women present?

Jesus was not a true revolutionary in the political sense. He was not dry wood sparking a fire of revolt. His was a spiritual kingdom. Yes, it would vastly influence the politics of a nation, but not in the rebellious way that those in power feared. He ushered in a kingdom of peace and yet was being tortured and crucified. What would happen when Israel truly rebelled against Rome? This is Jesus' question to them. He was warning them that by rejecting the Messiah, they were bringing judgment on themselves. Jesus' words of warning came true in AD 70.

Read aloud Luke 23:32–43.

What was the name of the place where Jesus was crucified?

The Latin word *calvaria* means skull. It is only presumed where this location actually was near Jerusalem, but it is from this word that we get our familiar Christian term "Calvary" for the place of Jesus' death. Some translations of the Bible refer to this place as Golgotha. This is the same word, skull, in Aramaic. It is a reference to the shape of the hill where Jesus was crucified.

What did Jesus say about His executioners while hanging on the cross?

How do the taunts of the religious leaders echo the temptation of Satan in Luke 4:9–11?

How did the two criminals respond to Jesus?

What promise did Jesus offer the one criminal?

For Jesus to tell the thief that He had authority to take him into paradise meant His authority was equivalent to God's as judge over the thief's righteousness. This thief had been condemned as a criminal who stated himself that he deserved to die (see v. 41). Jesus' gracious offer of pardon stands in stunning contrast to the horror of hanging on a cross in brutal sentencing.

Read aloud Luke 23:44–49.
What time in the day is it now?

What did it look like outside?

What happened inside the temple?

According to Luke, what were the last spoken words of Jesus on the cross?

What conclusion did the Roman centurion reach as he witnessed Jesus' death?

How did the crowd respond?

What did Jesus' followers do?

The sixth hour would have been noon. Jesus called this the hour of darkness in the garden of Gethsemane, and it literally became so! Darkness covered the earth and the veil tore in two. This veil separated the Holy of Holies—the inner room of the temple—from the Holy Place, the outer chamber.

When we read about Zechariah entering the temple to burn incense and Gabriel appearing to him, this would have been in the Holy Place. Beyond the veil in the Holy of Holies was where the Shekinah Glory, or very presence of God, dwelt. No one could see God and live. Only once a year, on the Day of Atonement, would the High Priest enter the Holy of Holies to sprinkle blood on the mercy seat of the Ark of the Covenant. In fact, according to rabbinic writings, they would fasten a bell and a rope around the ankle of the High Priest in the event God struck Him dead. The bell would ring at his fall, and they would pull him out with a rope, so no other priest would enter the Holy of Holies to remove him.

According to Hebrews 9:11–14, how is Christ's sacrifice on the cross superior to the annual sacrifice of the High Priest? What do we gain from this sacrifice?

Here within these last two verses of today's reading we discover three responses to Jesus:

- The centurion *praised God.*
- The people *went away beating their breasts.*
- Jesus' followers *watched from a distance.*

When we discuss Jesus' death for our sins today, we see these same three responses. Some people accept Jesus' payment for sin and praise God. Others may walk away in a moment of penitence that an innocent man died, but have no lasting conversion in their lives to follow Jesus' teaching and truth. Others watch from a distance, unsure exactly what this death of Jesus means for them.

Notice that none of these reactions represent how we *feel* about Jesus. Whether we *think* Him kind, good, or giving. Rather, they all represent how we respond to Him—in thought, deed, and choice. *These responses depict our reaction and subsequent action in response to Jesus' death.* The writer of Hebrews informs us that Jesus' sacrifice not only atones for our sins, it clears our consciences. In other words, it should alter both our decisions and our deeds.

Which reaction indicates your response to Jesus?

WEEK 8 | DAY 3
A DIM LIGHT DAWNING
LUKE 23:50–24:12

Today we are going to meet people whose decisions and deeds separated them from the crowd. Their courage propelled them into action. Today we will meet those who chose to honor Jesus despite their disillusionment and disappointment over the current circumstances.

Read aloud Luke 23:50–56.

How does Luke describe Joseph of Arimathea?

Finish this description of him in verse 51: who had not consented to their _____ and _____ ; and he was looking for the kingdom of God.

These two words are the core of how every one of us on the planet will respond to Jesus. We will make decisions as to what we believe about Jesus, which will lead to certain actions. Or inaction. But whatever decision we make, it will alter the course of our lives. Joseph's beliefs about Jesus led him to take a very risky action.

To whom did Joseph go to inquire about Jesus' body?

Since Jesus had been executed as an insurrectionist against Rome and since Joseph served as a member of the ruling council, what risks would such action involve?

What did Joseph do with Jesus' body?

Who followed him to the tomb?

What special Jewish day was about to begin?

What additional information do we get about the tomb in Matthew 27:57–61?

Never one to throw in extraneous details, Luke makes sure we understand that there was no possible way Jesus' tomb could have been confused with anyone else's. Nor His body. In first-century Palestine, several bodies would be wrapped in linens and perfumes and laid within the same tomb. After several months, when the flesh would have finished decaying, the family and friends would return to the tomb to collect the bones of their deceased loved ones, and they would be placed within a burial site where all their ancestral bones were kept.

The women sought to honor Jesus by following their Jewish customs in properly anointing and wrapping His body after His death. This also lets us know of their courage, as their presence at the tomb of Jesus would quickly and readily mark them as followers of His and potentially put them in great danger. Yet these women who had faithfully honored Him in His life and ministry continued to bravely honor Him in His death as well.

The problem, however, was that the Sabbath was beginning, and they could not perform the burial rites according to the commandment to do no work on this day. Jews marked the Sabbath beginning at sundown as well as a new day starting. The daytime of the Sabbath was called the Day of Preparation, and according to Jewish calculations, would still constitute the day prior.

There are various theories regarding what day of the week Jesus was crucified with compelling arguments as to how the gospel writers calculated the "three days."[33] It's interesting to consider various scholars' viewpoints!

Read aloud Luke 24:1–12.
What day did the women return?

According to Matthew 27:62–66, who would they have been prepared to encounter on returning?

Based on what you know of Roman history and how the soldiers had treated Jesus during His trials before Pilate and Herod, how dangerous do you think this would have been for unaccompanied women?

What problem did they consider? See Mark 16:1–3.

However, when they arrived they saw that this problem had been solved. What had happened according to Luke 24:2 and Matthew 28:1–4?

What was missing?

How did the women feel?

Who appeared to them?

What did these angels announce?

Where did the women go next?

How did the disciples respond to their story?

Who returned to the tomb for further investigation?

According to John 20:11–18, to whom did Jesus appear first?

I find it so beautiful that this brave and loving soul was the first to behold her risen Savior. They would have expected to have to face the Roman soldiers and beseech their permission to attend to Jesus. Even though in their minds at this time, their beloved Jesus was dead and would have no knowledge of their great act of service to Him in a proper burial or love for Him in exhibiting such potential risk, these brave and compassionate souls faithfully trekked toward the tomb, no doubt wondering what they would face from their Roman oppressors upon their arrival. The one who willingly risked the rejection of the apostles in insisting she had seen angels. The one who returned to the strange scene yet a second time, confused, dazed, and heartbroken, yet unwilling to give up her search for her Savior's body. What boundless courage! What resolve of purpose! Even in her grief and disappointment she sought one thing only: to be in the presence of her Savior. Even when He seemingly had no life left to offer her.

Have you ever been in a situation where you felt as though not even Jesus had any life left to offer you? What emotions did you experience, and what decisions did you make?

The truth is that nearly all of us will go through a season or circumstance of life in which the presence of Jesus seems missing or strangely silent. We will wonder where He has gone. What it all means. And why life is happening as it is. We will think, "It isn't supposed to be this way!" or "I would never have chosen this, and why is God allowing this to happen?" We will weep, face down in despair, just like Mary.

Until we hear Him whisper our name. And we will want to cling to Him with every fiber of our being. And He will speak, reminding us who He is and what

He promises to do. He will give us direction, a purpose in the midst of the pain. And we will rise in our sorrow and remind others of those promises. Who are you seeking today in your bewilderment, doubt, or despair? Is it Jesus? He will come to you, just as He came to Mary.

Based on Mary's actions, the words of the angels, and her grief, do you think Mary had understood that Jesus was going to rise from the dead?

Based on the disciples' reaction to her news, do you think the disciples expected Him to be resurrected?

Have you forgotten you serve a risen Christ? Remember, where life feels dull, dreary, or dead, you serve the God who raises the dead! We don't have to understand it all. We don't need all the "whys" answered. We don't need all our tears dried. We just need to seek Jesus. And He will come in our darkest hours and bring His light and life, even in the bleakest of days and the blackest of nights. Always.

BURNING HEARTS

LUKE 24:13–49

When the women returned from the tomb and told the disciples about the angels who had appeared to them and that Jesus' body was gone, we are told the disciples considered this an idle tale. What is important to note, however, is that it did lead to action from two of the disciples. Peter and John decided to go take a look, even though they doubted. We aren't told if they were simply curious or if the women's report triggered a memory of what Jesus had previously said. We are only told they both got up and ran to the tomb themselves.

While our own faith in encountering the risen Christ may not lead others to immediate belief themselves, it can spur them on to seek some answers. Or discover some additional facts. And dig more deeply. Take a look themselves at the evidence. And should they seek, God in His great mercy will provide opportunity for them to encounter the risen Christ as well.

Read aloud Luke 24:13–27.
What question did Cleopas ask Jesus?

What does this simple question imply about how widespread the knowledge of Jesus' death and resurrection was?

According to these two, who exactly had instigated Jesus' crucifixion?

Who had seen the risen Jesus, according to these disciples?

How did Jesus respond to their news? What did He begin to do?

Why do you suppose Jesus decided to conceal His identity while explaining the Scriptures to them?

I find it interesting that they make absolutely no mention of Mary Magdalene's claim to have beheld the risen Christ. The resurrection of Christ still baffles them. All they speak of is the angelic appearance before the group of women who had gone to the tomb to anoint His body and found Him missing.

Read aloud Luke 24:28–35.
What did Jesus do as they sat down at the table?

What happened in that moment?

What did Jesus do?

What reaction did they affirm with each other?

What did they immediately do?

Who else had seen the risen Lord at this point?

We are not explicitly told in the gospel accounts how Jesus' encounter with Peter had occurred. We are only told that He was the first apostle to whom He appeared. The beauty of this encounter with Cleopas and his companion on the road to Emmaus informs us of several possible ways in which we may encounter Jesus ourselves.

We are told that these two disciples were discussing Jesus while traveling. Jesus concealed His identity from them, probably so they would pay attention to His teaching rather than marvel at His presence. He then explained to them the words of Moses, the prophets, and all the Scriptures concerning Himself.

The first means by which we encounter Jesus is through His Word. The Word speaks of Him and testifies to His person, His purpose, and His plan.

Next, we are told that their eyes were opened when Jesus blessed the bread, broke it, and gave it to them. It is in the partaking of the holy sacrament of Communion, as our Lord commanded us to do in remembrance of Him, that we see our Savior clearly. We commemorate His person: He is our sacrifice. His purpose: He is our salvation. His plan: our surrender to obey Him as our King and invite others into this glorious kingdom.

Last, in their excitement, they immediately returned to Jerusalem, risking the danger of nighttime travel, to rejoin the disciples and share their joy. Upon their arrival they learn that Jesus also had appeared to Peter. It is in the testimony and joy of our fellow followers that we encounter Jesus.

His person: the Risen Living Lord. His purpose: to bring life to all people. His plan: to reveal Himself to the world through His followers.

Through the Scriptures.
Through the breaking of bread.
Through the fellowship.

How do we see this lived out in Acts 2:42–43, and what result did it bring?

Awe had already come over Mary's soul. Then Peter's. Now over Cleopas and his traveling companion. We do not have to see the physical body of the risen Christ to be filled with awe. Instead, we are invited to encounter His marvelous presence through the practices of Acts 2:42–43.

Which of these practices are easiest for you? Which are harder? Why?

Read aloud Luke 24:33–49.
To whom did Jesus appear next?

What did they think they were seeing?

Why would Jesus eating in front of them prove He was not merely a spirit or ghost?

What did Jesus explain to them, and how were they made able to understand it?

What else was Jesus going to do to enable them to proclaim to all nations His ability to forgive sins?

How does Jesus describe the power that was to come from on high in John 16:7–8, 13?

The Spirit of truth, the Holy Spirit, has come, and He lives within those of us who profess Jesus as our Lord and Savior. He promises to reveal to us the Scripture and make us witnesses of the truth of Christ's death and resurrection. When was the last time you intentionally tapped into that incredible power and wisdom that resides within you?

WEEK 8 | DAY 5

BOLD TONGUES

LUKE 24:50–52; ACTS 1:1–11

I remember that day at church all too well. There was an urgency within our office, but no one addressed it. A flurry of activity, but most of us knew not why. We sensed something big was happening, but no one could put their finger on what it was. Then our pastor called us all together and filled us in: he had accepted a call to another church and would no longer be pastoring ours.

My heart sank. Yet, I was also thrilled God was opening this opportunity for him. He needed a change. And rest from heading up our burgeoning church plant. Suddenly we all were in the know, and yet we were still left with a thousand questions running through our minds.

I imagine this is how the disciples must have felt. Jesus explained how the Scriptures foretold of His death and resurrection. They understood that they were to take these facts and share them with others. They were certain He was indeed the Messiah, the Son of God. They had been witnesses of all He had said and done. But still a million questions. And so it is in our own life of faith. Jesus clearly leads us to a certain point and then places us under the guidance of the Holy Spirit to continue the rest of our faith journey until His return.

Read aloud Luke 24:50–52.

Where did Jesus lead them, and what did He do for them while there?

Where did Jesus go next?

What did the disciples do?

This exchange doesn't lead us to believe they now had all the answers as to what it meant to be Jesus' witnesses. They merely obeyed what Jesus had told them to do next: return to Jerusalem and wait.

This is such a great reminder for us when our own path seems unclear. In those moments of uncertainty, Jesus calls us to worship, wait, and willingly obey. He doesn't ask us to wring our hands with worry or woefully wonder when He will provide a direct answer to our query.

What He does ask us to do is worship with joy that He has a plan and a purpose that He is intentionally unfolding and fulfilling in His perfect time.

He also asks us to willingly obey what He has already made clear to do in His Word.

He asks us to wait.

The disciples did not know exactly when the Holy Spirit was going to arrive. There is nothing in any of the gospel accounts, the book of Acts, nor the apostles' letters to the churches leading us to believe they knew exactly what was going to happen next in their lives as Jesus' chosen witnesses. They were simply told to wait. We are waiting on a risen Savior who holds all power and authority over our questions and our circumstances.

What is an area of your life in which the future feels tenuous or uncertain?

What is most difficult for you in this moment: to worship, willingly obey, or wait?

Why do you find it so difficult?

Why do you think Jesus unveils His plans to us slowly rather than all at once?

The next phase of the disciples' instruction begins in Acts, right where Luke's gospel ends. Thus begins the story of how Unexplainable Jesus offers the disciples an Unexplainable Life.

Jesus explained from a practical standpoint why we cannot know the exact time of His return. If they knew His return was imminent, they may decide to sit around in ease, just waiting instead of working. And Jesus had given them work to do—they were to take His gospel to the ends of the earth.

The other problem with knowing could be the opposite. They might feel that God made them wait too long, so they would give up and quit the mission. Jesus immediately jumps into several discourses emphasizing that they must be prepared and ready for His arrival at any moment. While they wait, they must eagerly be about His call on their lives.

Read aloud Matthew 25:1–13.
What might be some practical ways to ensure we have prepared ourselves with adequate oil while we wait for Christ's return?

"Christ will come when least expected—at midnight—and when the Church, having become accustomed to His long delay, has gone to sleep. So sudden will be His coming, that after the cry of announcement there will not be time for anything but to go forth and meet Him; it is impossible in the day of Christ's coming to make up for neglect of previous preparation."[34]

And so we, like the disciples, worship, willingly obey what we know we have been called to do, and wait with eagerness for the return of our bridegroom.
It was Mary Magdalene who was the first to witness His resurrection.

Jesus promises that when He returns again all will see Him as one sees a flash across the sky.

It was Mary who demonstrated blind faith that Jesus had returned from the dead, fell on her feet before Him in worship, and willingly obeyed Him, returning to tell the others, despite their dismissal of her. She modeled such faith and joy to men marred by doubt and confusion. Ought we not to follow in her footsteps and adopt such great faith ourselves?

We know not the day nor the hour, but could it be our Savior longs to appear to His children today—maybe not in a flash across the sky, but instead within the caverns of our hearts, the cracks and crevices within our souls, and the questions within our circumstances—to reveal to us the mysteries of His glorious appearing and call us to announce, "He is risen! The bridegroom is coming!"

Are we seeking Him? Preparing ourselves for Him to come and work within us as we wait for His final arrival?

Mary was the first to experience His resurrection. Let us, O children of this great and glorious King, be the first to experience His revival.

Come, Unexplainable Jesus. Your children stand ready to receive you with joy.

CONTINUING THE JOURNEY

My prayer for you, for all of us, at the beginning of this study was that you would experience a bold new encounter with Christ. You would discover, or perhaps rediscover, how unexplainable He truly is. His teaching, His claims, His miracles, His death and resurrection, and His call on your own heart and life to follow Him.

I pray you have been awakened to the incredible love of your Savior as never before.

For some of you, there may still be questions. Dr. Luke may have helped you arrive at his same diagnosis of Jesus: the human and divine Messiah, come to save the world! However, you may be grappling with what following Him looks like in your time and place and circumstances. If so, I would invite you to consider joining me through the study *An Unexplainable Life*. Here is an excerpt to get you thinking:

> By diligently researching all the facts regarding Jesus, he (Luke) arrives at his verdict: "You may have certainty concerning the things you have been taught" (Luke 1:4). Jesus is indeed the Christ. By the end of the book of Luke, he is firm in this conclusion. From there, he moves on to Acts: the treatment plan. Acts lays out for Theophilus the steps that the followers of Jesus took based on their conclusion that Jesus was indeed the promised Messiah. It is the treatment plan for a disciple.
>
> In a physician's mind, a diagnosis is meaningless if the patient remains untreated. It is the treatment plan that makes the knowledge of the diagnosis worthwhile. Thus it is for Luke: "I have dealt with all that Jesus **began** to do and teach" (Acts 1:1, emphasis mine). Keep reading, Theophilus. We're talking about more than just an intellectual understanding that Jesus is the Messiah. Did you get that, friend? Accepting Jesus as your Savior is just the beginning . . .

I don't know if you're closing this book today feeling as though you are currently walking a dry and dusty road, standing on a glorious mountaintop, hanging on for dear life in a storm-tossed sea, or gasping for air in the valley of the shadow of death, but what I do know is that Jesus is with you in any and every circumstance. I also know He invites you to go with Him on the grandest adventure of your life. There will never be another today. Unexplainable Jesus holds out His nail-scarred hand, pierces into your very soul with His calm yet resolute gaze. A grin flashes across His face and He whispers, "Come, follow Me!"

NOTES

Week Two: Unexplainable Birth

1. About the status of shepherds, Craig Keener says, " . . . this narrative (Luke 2:8–20) would have challenged the values of many religious people, who despised shepherds (the earlier examples of Moses and David notwithstanding); shepherds' work kept them from participation in the religious activities of their communities. More clearly, elites throughout the empire usually viewed contemporary shepherds negatively" (Craig S. Keener, *The IVP Bible Background Commentary: New Testament* [Downers Grove, IL: IVP Academic, 2014], 185).

2. Gerhard Kittel and Gerhard Friedrich, eds., *Theological Dictionary of the New Testament* (Grand Rapids, MI: Eerdmans, 1964), 151.

3. Keener, *The IVP Bible Background Commentary: New Testament*, 264.

Week Three: Unexplainable Introductions

4. Keener, *The IVP Bible Background Commentary: New Testament*, 190.

5. Alfred Edersheim, *The Life and Times of Jesus the Messiah* (McLean, VA: MacDonald Publishing, 1886), 453.

6. Walter A. Elwell, and Barry J. Beitzel, eds., "Apostle, Apostleship," in *Baker Encyclopedia of the Bible*, vol. 1 (Grand Rapids: Baker Book House, 1988), 131–32.

7. Ibid., 132–33.

8. Keener, *The IVP Bible Background Commentary: New Testament*, 90.

Week Four: Unexplainable Teaching

9. I. Howard Marshall, A. R. Millard, J. I. Packer, D. J. Wiseman, eds., "good," in *New Bible Dictionary*, 3rd ed. (Leicester, England; Downers Grove, IL: InterVarsity Press, 1996), 424.

10. Gerhard Kittel and Gerhard Friedrich, eds., "existemi," in *Theological Dictionary of the New Testament,* trans. Geoffrey W. Bromily, elec. ed., vol. 2 (Grand Rapids: Eerdmans, 1964), 459.

11. Philip Yancey, *Rumors of Another World: What on Earth Are We Missing?* (Grand Rapids: Zondervan, 2003), 187.

12. Kenneth E. Bailey, *Poet & Peasant and Through Peasant Eyes: A Literary-Cultural Approach to the Parables in Luke* (Grand Rapids: Eerdmans, 1983), 46.

13. Ibid., 55.

14. N. T. Wright, *Luke for Everyone* (Louisville: Westminster John Knox Press, 2004), 131.

15. Bailey, *Poet & Peasant and Through Peasant Eyes,* 123.

Week Five: An Unexplainable Kingdom

16. *Merriam-Webster*, s.v. "covetous," https://www.merriam-webster.com/dictionary/covetous.

17. Bailey, *Poet & Peasant and Through Peasant Eyes*, 152–53.

18. Ibid., 154.

19. N. T. Wright, *Luke for Everyone*, 184.

20. Bailey, *Poet & Peasant and Through Peasant Eyes*, 100.
21. Ibid., 102.

Week Six: Unexplainable Invitations

22. Elwell and Beitzel, "Master," *Baker Encyclopedia of the Bible*, vol. 2, 1416.
23. John F. Walvoord and Roy B. Zuck, *The Bible Knowledge Commentary New Testament* (Colorado Springs: David C. Cook, 1983), 67.

Week Seven: Unexplainable Confrontations

24. James Swanson, *Dictionary of Biblical Languages with Semantic Domains: Greek (New Testament)* (Oak Harbor, WA: Logos Research Systems, Inc., 1997).
25. Ibid.
26. Keener, *The IVP Bible Background Commentary: New Testament*, 233–34.
27. Charles Caldwell Ryrie, *The Ryrie Study Bible* (Chicago: Moody, 2011), 1272, note for Luke 21:7.
28. Keener, *The IVP Bible Background Commentary: New Testament*, 235.
29. Ceil and Moishe Rosen, *Christ in the Passover* (Chicago: Moody, 2006), 64.
30. Ibid., 65.
31. Ibid.
32. Ibid., 22.

Week Eight: An Unexplainable Rescue

33. "On what day was Jesus crucified?," Got Questions, https://www.gotquestions.org/three-days.html.
34. Alfred Edersheim, *The Life and Times of Jesus the Messiah,* 458–59.

ACKNOWLEDGMENTS

Unexplainable Jesus—never in a hundred million years could I feel worthy to write words to describe You. My only comfort is my sincere belief that You wrote these words through me.

My family: Jonathan, Eliana, and Nathan, my heart and world. Your patience and sacrifice in allowing this work to be done deserves great applause.

My grandparents, Jack and Valois, who first showed me what following Jesus looks like.

My pastor, Steve Engram, who brings all of us at Desert Springs Community Church to the feet of Jesus every Sunday. How grateful I am for your shepherding.

My church family, how grateful I am to come home on Sundays.

My prayer warriors, always a text or post away, you keep me going when the road got long and dusty and I wanted to abandon the journey.

My chief prayer warrior, Tami—how grateful I am for your partnership in ministry and your friendship in life. My mentor, Sharon—always pointing me back to what matters most. Jen—I'd have to write another book for all the ways you've blessed my life.

Judy Dunagan, whose very presence ushers you to the feet of Jesus. May all I have learned from you be stewarded well and with excellence. Your ability to take my emotional exuberance and put it into something meaningful is no small feat!

Pam Pugh, I can think of no other person on the planet with whom I'd rather unravel pages of theology with prayerful consideration! It is with highest esteem and deepest gratitude I pore through your questions and suggestions. Thank you for patiently sharpening the words of this study to present each point with clarity.

To every seeker or follower of Jesus. I pray you saw the Savior a little more clearly, fell in love with Him a little more deeply, and surrendered your soul to Him fully, because there is no other journey more worth taking than the Road of this Rabbi. See you at the throne, my friend!

What can God do with fifty days?

An Unexplainable Life is a call to reignite the mission and movement of the early church individually and collectively. This in-depth, 10-week Bible study challenges our modern-day assumptions, inspires us to reclaim the zeal of the apostles, and invites us to join Jesus in His work today.

978-0-8024-1473-1 | also available as an eBook

MOODY
Publishers®

From the Word to Life®

Will you accept a divine invitation?

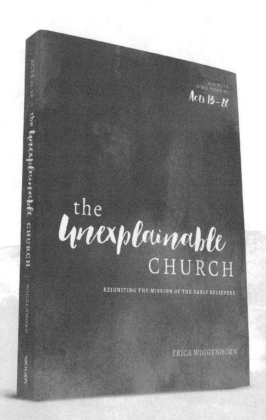

The Unexplainable Church is a 10-week inductive study of Acts 13–28 that features scholarly insights, personal reflections, and prompts for application. It will teach by example how to study the Bible deeply, and it will challenge you toward critical life-change: submitting your will to the mission of the church, where life finds its fullest meaning.

978-0-8024-1742-8 | also available as an eBook

MOODY
Publishers®

From the Word to Life®

Bible Studies for Women

IN-DEPTH. CHRIST-CENTERED. REAL IMPACT.

AN UNEXPLAINABLE LIFE
978-0-8024-1473-1

THE UNEXPLAINABLE CHURCH
978-0-8024-1742-8

HIS LAST WORDS
978-0-8024-1467-0

I AM FOUND
978-0-8024-1468-7

INCLUDED IN CHRIST
978-0-8024-1591-2

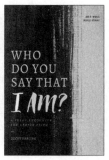

THIS I KNOW
978-0-8024-1596-7

WHO DO YOU SAY THAT I AM?
978-0-8024-1550-9

HE IS ENOUGH
978-0-8024-1686-5

IF GOD IS FOR US
978-0-8024-1713-8

ON BENDED KNEE
978-0-8024-1919-4

MOODY
Publishers®

From the Word to Life®

Explore our Bible studies at
moodypublisherswomen.com

Also available as eBooks